PLANNING AND MARKETING CONFERENCES AND WORKSHOPS

Robert G. Simerly

PLANNING AND MARKETING CONFERENCES AND WORKSHOPS

Tips, Tools, and Techniques

Jossey-Bass Publishers

San Francisco • Oxford • 1990

PLANNING AND MARKETING CONFERENCES AND WORKSHOPS
Tips, Tools, and Techniques
by Robert G. Simerly

Copyright ©1990 by: Jossey-Bass Inc., Publishers
350 Sansome Street
San Francisco, California 94104
&
Jossey-Bass Limited
Headington Hill Hall
Oxford OX3 0BW

Library of Congress Cataloging-in-Publication Data

Simerly, Robert G.
  Planning and marketing conferences and workshops : tips, tools, and techniques / Robert G. Simerly.
       p.   cm. — (A joint publication in the Jossey-Bass management series and the Jossey-Bass higher education series)
  Includes bibliographical references.
  ISBN 1-55542-235-7
  1. Meetings—Planning—Handbooks, manuals, etc.   2. Congresses and conventions—Planning—Handbooks, manuals, etc.   I. Title.
 II. Series: Jossey-Bass higher education series.   III. Series: Jossey-Bass management series.
  AS6.S546   1990
  658.4′56—dc20   89-49493
                                                                              CIP

Manufactured in the United States of America

The paper in this book meets the guidelines for permanence and durability of the Committee on Production Guidelines for Book Longevity of the Council on Library Resources.

JACKET DESIGN BY WILLI BAUM

FIRST EDITION

Code 9035

A joint publication in
The Jossey-Bass Management Series
and
The Jossey-Bass
Higher Education Series

Consulting Editor
Adult and Continuing Education

Alan B. Knox
University of Wisconsin, Madison

Contents

Preface

Several years ago over dinner, a friend and I were discussing the complex activity of planning and marketing conferences and workshops. We calculated that in more than twenty years' experience in continuing education, I have provided the administrative leadership for organizations that have planned upwards of 8,000 conferences and workshops. My friend suggested, "Since this is such a complicated business, why don't you write about your experience? Over the years you've developed many practical tips and guidelines and learned what to do and what not to do during planning. And you've developed a research base for marketing activities that can be translated into very practical terms for people planning conferences and workshops." And that is how this book was conceived.

Planning and Marketing Conferences and Workshops builds on a research and knowledge base acquired during the planning and marketing of those 8,000 conferences and workshops. I take what is known about excellence in professional practice and distill that experience and wisdom into a series of practical pointers that you can put to work immediately.

Who Should Read This Book

No matter what the setting of the conference or workshop you are planning, you will find here a wealth of practical advice in the form of short, easy-to-implement tips. Conference organizers in the following categories will find the tips especially valuable:

- Professional associations that plan conferences and workshops for their members
- Providers of continuing education programs in colleges and universities
- Cooperative extension staff in land-grant universities
- Businesses that plan public conferences and workshops
- Governmental agencies that use direct-mail advertising for educational programs

- Fraternal and religious organizations that plan conferences and workshops for their members
- Businesses that contract to run conferences and workshops for clients

Corporate meeting planners are another group of readers who will benefit from the book. Since these planners already have a built-in audience, they may not find all the tips on marketing programs applicable, but they will be able to use the tips on planning and evaluating programs, negotiating contracts for meeting space, producing excellence in graphic design to enhance the corporate image, and managing budgets. In addition, Chapter Eight contains a list of the latest resources for successful planning and marketing of conferences and workshops.

In short, those who have responsibility for planning almost any type of conference or workshop will find this book an invaluable guide, because of the interdisciplinary, practical nature of the tips provided here.

Overview of the Contents

Chapter One contains eighteen tips for program design and development. In it I analyze why it is important to distinguish between advisory and planning committees, and I include sample letters for inviting people to serve on either type of committee. A sample script for telephone interviews with potential attendees can quickly be adapted to meet your specific needs and will help you structure program content. Tips are given for redesigning existing programs so that they can be offered on a special in-house basis to clients. This chapter contains a sample form for conducting a needs assessment for in-house programs and an instrument to use in surveying program attendees for suggestions about future program development. The first chapter concludes with a comprehensive twenty-six-point checklist to consider during program development.

Chapter Two analyzes thirty-four tips for selecting, maintaining, and tracking mailing lists. It contains names and addresses of sources for mailing lists, tips on how to secure certain mailing lists without charge, and advice on using list brokers. Practical advice is offered on merging lists to purge duplicate names, along with guidelines on how to handle the duplicate name problem if you cannot afford a computerized merge/purge process. I also provide tips for simplifying the process of updating your internal mailing list, with sample forms for conducting such an update. I explain how to analyze, after a program is over, how effective each list was in relation to the cost of obtaining the names and mailing to the list. In addition, I present a cost-benefit spreadsheet, which can be adapted for a personal computer, for analyzing the return on your direct-mail advertising. Like all the forms throughout the book, it can easily be modified to meet your individual needs. At the end of the chapter is a twenty-two-point checklist designed to improve selection, maintenance, and tracking of mailing lists.

Chapter Three contains thirty-one tips related to graphic design, typesetting, and printing: All of these elements contribute to achieving a quality image for your organization and its programs. Besides a sample letter of agreement to use when hiring graphic designers, there are hints on how to work with them. Other tips discuss what typefaces and type size to use in direct-mail advertising. I analyze the importance of color and give advice on how to select the appropriate ink colors to convey a quality image. Money-saving tips on how to achieve the look of multiple colors while only using one color, guidelines on the use of photographs and illustrations, and advice on selecting color of paper stock are all provided, as are hints on how to slash your typesetting bill in half. The chapter concludes with a thirty-point checklist to help you effectively establish a quality image for your organization and its programs.

Chapter Four is devoted to the budget design and planning process. It is written for the person who, though required to manage budgets, has never had an accounting course. I list twenty-eight tips for developing accurate and realistic budgets and, to simplify the budgeting process, provide an easy-to-use budget form that is equally effective for small or large programs and can be modified readily, as necessary. I demonstrate why it is imperative to distinguish between fixed and variable costs, as you can easily do using the sample budget form. The tips explain how to recover administrative costs through a charge-back system that is reflected in the registration fee for a program. A sample spreadsheet for planning an entire year of programs is included to demonstrate how to calculate the administrative fee for individual programs, so that you can meet your overall office expenses. Illustrations of sample budget printouts show how to present a summary of income and expenses in such a way that all the key players in the program can understand it. Review the thirteen-point checklist at the end of the chapter as you plan any upcoming budgets.

Negotiating favorable contracts for meeting space, lodging, and meals is the topic of Chapter Five. Seventeen tips help you simplify the process and ensure excellence in this important area of planning conferences and workshops. Sample contracts illustrate the do's and don't's of drawing up a contract, and tips explain how to avoid being taken advantage of during contract negotiations. You can save substantial amounts of money by following the tips on negotiating for additional services when you reserve a meeting space. Further tips help you plan meal functions that contribute to the overall success of your program. A checklist of sixteen important items to review in connection with booking space, lodging, and meals is located at the end of the chapter.

In Chapter Six I discuss the complex process of evaluating and improving programs and recommend evaluation techniques that have proved to be practical, easy, and economical to implement. I explain the difference between formative and summative evaluation and provide guidelines on how to use each effectively. Six different sample evaluation instruments are included, with a comprehensive analysis of when to use each type of instrument. I explain in detail how to avoid the mistakes most often made in evaluating programs. There are also tips on how to link evaluation with market research. The checklist at the end of the chapter contains sixteen items to review as you plan any evaluation.

Chapter Seven's twenty-six practical, easy-to-implement tips relate to conducting market research and analysis. Guidelines are given for what to include in a comprehensive data base for market research in your organization. I explain a simple approach to conducting a market audit and list tips on quick ways to research your competition. Forms to use in conducting market research cover such important areas as how to survey your customers' image of your organization and how to find out why people did not register for your programs. The tips emphasize the importance of using both quantitative and qualitative data for market research. The end-of-the-chapter checklist of twenty-one important items to review in conducting action-oriented research is designed to keep you and your organization on the cutting edge of excellence.

The last chapter contains a complete list of key resources and readings for conference and workshop planners — for example, the major suppliers of audiovisual equipment for your programs and a list of computer software helpful in running a conference office — software to assist you in accounting for income and expenses and in writing personalized letters to increase your marketing effectiveness. The chapter also contains suggestions on conferences, workshops, and meetings to attend for professional development. Catalogues of conference and office supplies and equipment are listed, as are sources for ordering films and both large and small display systems, magazines helpful in conference planning, and sources for promotional supplies, visual charts, and control and calendar systems. Also included are names and addresses of professional organizations that assist people in planning conferences and workshops. The chapter concludes with a comprehensive bibliography of additional books related to planning and marketing successful conferences and workshops.

Acknowledgments

I am grateful to the many people who through the years have helped me learn how to run successful conferences and workshops, and I am especially indebted to the staff at the University of Nebraska, Lincoln, who are such excellent professionals that it is a joy to go to work in the morning. The exciting organizational climate they create serves as a dynamic laboratory for constant testing of new ideas related to meeting planning.

I am also grateful to my two secretaries, Peggy Flynn and Dee Leonard, who have worked tirelessly with me in producing the many drafts of the manuscript that resulted in this book. Their suggestions, cheerful dispositions, and professional skills have been indispensable throughout this project.

I appreciate Alan Knox's very helpful reading of the manuscript and suggestions for clarifying the ideas expressed in it.

Lynn Luckow at Jossey-Bass deserves special thanks for his guiding direction as editor. His counsel is always on target, considerate, and designed to improve the quality of thinking and writing. It is a pleasure to work with a professional of his calibre.

Last, I wish to thank my wife, Coby Bunch Simerly. She is my intellectual companion and best friend.

Lincoln, Nebraska   Robert G. Simerly
February 1990

The Author

Robert G. Simerly is dean of the Division of Continuing Studies and professor of adult education at the University of Nebraska, Lincoln. In this capacity he provides administrative leadership for a large continuing education organization with a staff of 150, serving 75,000 people each year throughout Nebraska and the rest of the United States and in more than 125 foreign countries.

Before assuming the position of dean at the University of Nebraska, Lincoln, Simerly was director of conferences and institutes at the University of Illinois, Urbana–Champaign, and before that, director of the Extended Campus program in the School of Education at Syracuse University. He has also held other teaching and administrative positions in higher education, as well as in public schools in the United States and Europe.

Simerly received his B.S. degree (1961) in education and English, his M.A. degree (1963) in liberal arts, with a major in English, and his Ed.D. degree (1973) in educational leadership, all from the University of Tennessee, Knoxville.

In addition to numerous articles, Simerly has written several books, including *Budgeting for Successful Conferences and Institutes* (1982), *Strategic Planning and Leadership in Continuing Education* (Simerly and Associates, 1987), and *Handbook of Marketing for Continuing Education* (Simerly and Associates, 1989).

The author is himself a popular workshop presenter. The workshops he has recently presented have covered such topics as practical marketing tips for continuing education organizations, how to increase registrations through effective marketing, strategic planning for the continuing education enterprise, successful financial management for continuing education organizations, how to write brochure copy that sells programs, organizational leadership effectiveness, how to empower staff for effective team building, strategic planning for organizational renewal, organizational conflict management, and improving communication skills. As a behavioral scientist, Simerly is particularly concerned with helping professionals in a wide variety of fields to enhance their personal and organizational effectiveness.

PLANNING AND MARKETING CONFERENCES AND WORKSHOPS

Introduction:

Fourteen Steps to Successful Conferences and Workshops

Planning successful conferences and workshops is a complex activity. This book has been written to provide assistance with this process through a series of practical, easy-to-implement tips. All of the tips provided have been tested by professionals. Many of these tips can be implemented immediately in your own organization, while others will need to be modified slightly to meet your individual needs.

Read through the tips, decide on the ones you should implement, and use the convenient checklists at the end of each chapter. All of the tips emphasize the importance of providing effective service, developing sound financial policies, engaging in creative program development, conducting effective evaluations, and using reliable and practical market research techniques.

Figure 1 shows fourteen important steps in developing conferences and workshops. The chapters in this book directly address all of these steps, which can be summarized as follows:

• *Step 1 — Idea for a program:* Program ideas come from many places. They come from reading articles and books, talking to people about their professional development needs, and studying what others are doing. Naturally not all ideas will prove to be marketable, which is why step 2 is so important.

Chapter One, entitled "Planning Dynamic Programs: Eighteen Tips for Program Design and Development," offers many practical ideas related to steps 1 to 8. The tips include guidelines, checklists, and special hints for implementation.

1

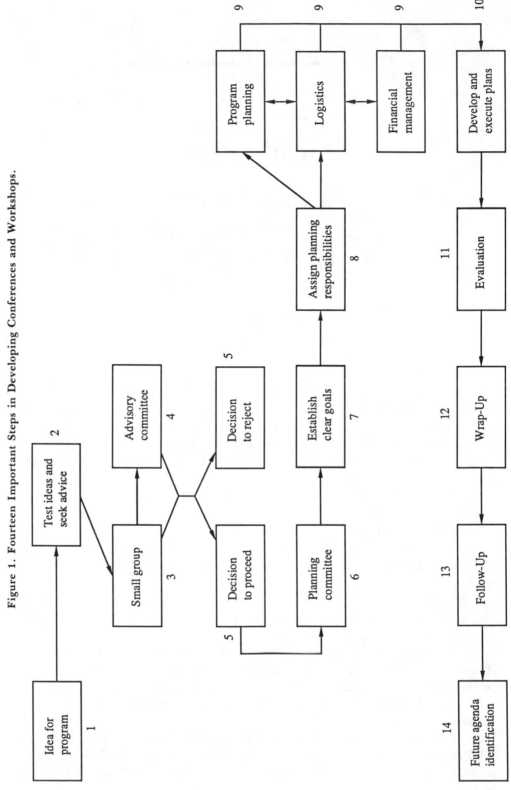

Figure 1. Fourteen Important Steps in Developing Conferences and Workshops.

- *Step 2 — Testing ideas and seeking advice:* It is essential to find out whether or not the basic idea for a program is marketable. An effective way to do this is through discussion and feedback from small groups and advisory committees, as described in the next two steps.

- *Step 3 — Small group feedback:* Small groups of people knowledgeable about the content of the program idea can provide information about the marketability of the idea. Through discussion and analysis with others, it is possible to explore the nuances of the content, the target group of potential attendees, and people who could serve as presenters.

- *Step 4 — Advisory committees:* Advisory committees are a more formal method for seeking reactions and suggestions about program ideas. Often a small group is first used to seek reactions. If these reactions are favorable, the next step is to create an advisory committee for further testing of ideas.

Using individuals and groups in the manner suggested in steps 1 to 4 is an effective way to engage in sophisticated market research. Chapter Seven describes in detail other strategies for conducting effective, practical market research designed to help you and your organization stay on the cutting edge.

- *Step 5 — Decision to proceed or reject:* After seeking advice and testing ideas, a decision is made either to proceed with the program idea or to reject it as being unsuitable at the present time. If the decision is to proceed, you move to the next step on the flowchart.

- *Step 6 — Planning committee:* This step may or may not be included, depending on your individual situation. If you are planning a small conference or workshop, often this step is omitted and you proceed with all the planning yourself. However, if you are planning a larger program, it is often appropriate to create a planning committee to assist with all aspects of the program planning.

- *Step 7 — Establishing clear goals:* This is one of the most important items in the planning process. All conferences and workshops should have clearly stated goals to guide the program development, marketing, administration, and evaluation.

Examples of how to establish and state goals are given in Chapters One and Six. Sample goals are stated, and an analysis is given on how to develop effective goal statements that can be successfully converted to powerful direct-mail advertising copy.

- *Step 8 — Assigning planning responsibilities:* Steps 9 and 10 deal with these specifics. During this step it is important to decide who is to be in charge of a program and to vest that person with the authority to make decisions regarding program, logistics, and financial management. *Hint:* Only one person and not more than one should be in charge in order to avoid potential misunderstandings later in the planning process.

- *Step 9 — Program planning, logistics, and financial management:* This step takes the clearly established goals and converts them into appropriate program content. Advisory and planning committees are often useful in providing advice in this area.

Chapter Two, entitled "Reaching Potential Participants: Thirty-Four Tips for Mailing List Selection, Maintenance, and Tracking," provides advice on how to avoid the most often made mistakes with mailing lists and mailing list tracking. Chapter Four provides tips on effective budgeting practices along with sample budget forms that are appropriate for both large and small programs. In Chapter Five, entitled "Negotiating Favorable Contracts: Seventeen Tips for Securing Meeting Space, Lodging, and Meals," the many tips include samples showing what should and should not be included in a contract.

- *Step 10 — Developing and executing plans:* This step recognizes that it is one thing to develop plans, and it is another to implement them. Plans that are made in step 9 are then unified and executed during step 10.

Chapter Three, entitled "Establishing a Quality Image: Thirty-One Tips for Graphic Design, Typesetting, and Printing," thoroughly analyzes this complex part of planning successful conferences and workshops.

- *Step 11 — Evaluation:* All conferences and workshops need to be evaluated in order to decide how successful they were. In addition, evaluation provides helpful information regarding plans for similar programs in the future.

Chapter Six is entitled "Evaluating and Improving Programs: Eighteen Tips for Determining Whether Programs Are Achieving Goals and Expectations." It contains a wide variety of useful evaluation forms and offers practical advice on how to conduct both formative and summative evaluation.

- *Step 12 — Wrap-up:* After a program is over, many details need to be attended to. This includes everything from writing thank-you letters to speakers and paying all bills to providing a final accounting of all income and expenses.

- *Step 13 — Follow-up:* This step concentrates on the analysis of issues such as the cost-effectiveness of all advertising. Developing effective tracking and analysis systems for this is covered in Chapter Two.

- *Step 14 — Future agenda identification:* This last important step concentrates on identifying things to do in relation to future programs. For example, it often includes identifying program content and presenters for future programs. It could also deal with repeating the program but marketing it in a different city.

This book provides a comprehensive overview and analysis of the success factors associated with planning and marketing effective conferences and workshops. The practical tips have been field-tested by a wide variety of professionals, and thus they represent excellence in professional practice.

Often the terms *marketing, advertising, publicity,* and *public relations* are used synonymously. However, for this book these four terms have separate and distinct meanings, as follows:

- *Marketing* is the two-way exchange process in which the organization and its customers both exchange something of value. Thus, this exchange involves people sending in registration fees in exchange for attendance at a program they perceive will be valuable to them. In addition, these clients will be exchanging another valuable commodity — the time required to participate in a program.

- *Advertising* is a subset of marketing and refers to any paid form of communication used by the organization to inform the public about its programs, products, and services. Typically, advertising uses such methods as direct-mail brochures and catalogues, ads in newspapers and magazines, radio and television ads, billboards, and flyers or posters.

- *Publicity* is also a subset of marketing. It refers to any nonpaid form of communication used to attract inquiries or registrations. Publicity often includes such activities as interviews on local radio and television talk shows, announcements in newsletters and organizational calendars, and news or feature stories in newspapers and magazines.

- *Public relations* is a subcomponent of publicity. However, there is one important difference as these terms are used in this book. Publicity is unpaid promotion that is highly targeted, while public relations is unpaid promotion that is generally not targeted to a specific audience. Rather, it is thought of as goodwill generated by the organization and staff. For example, staff who join civic groups are engaging in public relations efforts. Usually people have not highly targeted this area for marketing purposes, however. Rather, they use this as a way to network informally with people and thus create goodwill, for their organization and its programs.

Planners of conferences and workshops usually market their program through advertising and publicity. Then they use public relations to create overall goodwill.

For convenience's sake, the terms *conference* and *workshop* have been used throughout the book to refer to those activities that often are called by a variety of names — conferences, workshops, meetings, institutes, symposia, and forums.

As you read through the tips discussed in this book, think of how you might adapt them to your own programs. If a particular tip is not exactly right for your situation, consider modifying it to adapt it to your special requirements. All of the tips presented have actually been used successfully in a wide variety of public and private organizations, in both the profit and nonprofit sectors.

1

———————◆———————

Planning
Dynamic Programs:

Eighteen Tips for
Program Design and Development

Good program planning does not happen by accident. Rather, it is a result of a series of carefully thought-out strategies that consider the needs of the market and your own organization. The tips presented in this chapter will enable you to better plan the types of programs that will enhance the image of your organization, increase your registrations, bring in additional revenue, and provide effective service to participants. They emphasize the importance of planning, negotiating program expectations with key stakeholders, and conducting needs assessments to assist with program design.

Most important, each tip has been tested by professionals in the field. Read through the ideas, find the ones appropriate for your conferences and workshops, and modify these as needed to fit your specific needs.

Tip 1
Use planning and advisory committees to help develop programs.

Planning and advisory committees should be composed of representatives from the target group of potential registrants. These people are excellent sources for program development ideas. If you pick leaders in the field for committee membership, they usually are knowledgeable about new ideas that can be integrated into the content of your program design. They will often be acquainted with the leading experts who can be contacted to be presenters. They also know the special vocabulary and language related to the content, so this can be helpful as you write your advertising copy.

In addition, using planning and advisory committees can have valuable added side benefits. For example, they may volunteer to mention your

6

program during their upcoming speeches to community and civic groups. They may volunteer to distribute brochures at an annual meeting they will be attending. They may be available for radio and television interviews in which they talk about your program. If planning or advisory committee members have a genuine hand in providing input to shape excellent programming, they will want to ensure its success. Therefore, they are valuable not only for planning the program but also for marketing the program.

Tip 2
Clearly distinguish between advisory and planning committees.

Advisory committees are set up for what their name implies — to give you advice. You then make the decisions about the program. However, planning committees are designed to function differently. Usually their members are actually expected to help plan and sometimes even to help administer the program. Therefore, in order to avoid misunderstandings, clearly communicate three things as you recruit committee members: (1) exactly what type of committee you are creating, (2) what the duties of members are, and (3) what kind of time commitments will be required. These issues should be clarified when you ask people to accept your invitation to be on such a committee. They should also be restated in a follow-up letter. Exhibits 1 and 2 illustrate sample letters that clarify the distinction between planning committees and advisory committees.

**Exhibit 1. Letter of Invitation to Confirm
Membership on an Advisory Committee.**

Dear Ray:

This is a brief follow-up to my phone call requesting your services on the advisory committee for the next conference devoted to providing an economic update for business leaders in the state. This conference, which now has a five-year track record, attracts over 800 key business leaders each year.

The duties of the advisory committee are as follows:

- To give advice to our staff as we plan the conference. (We have established a luncheon meeting on November 8, from noon to 2:30, for our discussions.)
- To be available by telephone to our program planners for advice as they continue with the program development.
- To attend the conference on May 28.
- To be available for a postconference critique meeting that will be scheduled at a time mutually convenient for advisory committee members.

We appreciate your taking time out of your very busy schedule to help give us advice. Because of your input, we will be better able to design a conference attended by over 800 of our state's leaders in business, government, and industry.

Sincerely,

Robert G. Simerly

P.S. Enclosed are copies of brochures from the last five years. This will give you an idea of the topics that have been covered, who the presenters have been, and how the program has evolved over the years.

**Exhibit 2. Letter of Invitation for
Membership on a Planning Committee.**

Dear Carol:

I enjoyed our phone conversation last week, and I want to thank you for agreeing to be on the program planning committee of the Division of Conferences and Institutes for the upcoming national conference of the National University Continuing Education Association.

As I mentioned on the phone, the duties of planning committee members are as follows:

- To attend a planning committee meeting on September 10–11, in New York
- To attend a follow-up planning committee meeting on November 12–13, in Baltimore
- To attend the national conference in San Diego on April 7–10

As we discussed, this is very much a hands-on, working committee rather than just an advisory committee. Members will not only be planning the program; they will also be in charge of administering it. Because of your broad experience at running conferences and institutes, we will value your assistance.

We all appreciate the time you are willing to give to make this upcoming program a success. See you at the first meeting in New York. Additional details about the meeting times will be sent by May 10. In the meantime, if you have any questions, just give me a call.

Sincerely,

Robert G. Simerly

As can be seen from these two different examples in Exhibits 1 and 2, the expectations for committee membership are clearly spelled out in the letters of invitation. In addition, as noted in the letters, the expectations were first clarified in a conversation before the person accepted the committee membership. Therefore, the letters represent confirmations of agreements that had already been made.

Taking the time to clearly spell out these expectations should ensure that committee members understand exactly what is expected of them. For example, you do not want members of an advisory committee trying to change their roles and become conference planners. Similarly, you do not want planning committee members who need to plan as well as administer a program to abdicate these responsibilities and begin to see themselves as merely providers of advice while expecting someone else to do the work.

Tip 3
Begin the first advisory or planning committee meeting with an informal, welcoming activity.

This will give people a chance to get to know each other better before they have to begin working together. Setting a tone conducive to effective brainstorming and problem solving is important to the overall success of either type of committee. For the type of busy professional you want on your committees, often either breakfast, lunch, or dinner directly preceding the first meeting is a good choice. This activity does not have to be elaborate or long; it just needs to happen in a relaxed, informal, cordial manner. Doing this will go a long way toward paving the way to successful group discussion.

Tip 4
Give planning and advisory committee members a place on the program.

Obviously, it is not always appropriate to give planning or advisory committee members a major spot on the program. However, you can still tap their expertise by asking them to accept responsibility for such tasks as moderating discussions, participating in poster sessions, introducing speakers, making announcements, extending a welcome, giving short introductory and concluding remarks, and assisting with evaluations.

Becoming a part of the program can be an important psychological reward for their hard work on the committee. It also ensures that they will actually attend the program. Most people serving on planning and advisory committees expect to pay a registration fee for a program when they actually attend, so you can almost guarantee their registration. By virtue of having asked them to be on the committee in the first place, you are choosing recognized leaders with high visibility and credibility. Actively use this to reinforce the quality and excellence of your program. For example, you may find it useful to put the names and titles of committee members on a direct-mail brochure.

Tip 5
Conduct telephone interviews with potential attendees in order to help structure program content.

An effective way to develop excellent program content is to identify a list of ten people who are potential attendees for a program. Call them up, discuss your program ideas, and ask their advice. Most people, even busy executives, are willing to chat with you if you communicate a genuine need to get their input in order to do a better job of serving people like them. Rarely will they refuse to talk to you or be anything but cordial in assisting with thinking through program ideas.

There are three important keys to making these interviews work: (1) they must be conducted either by you or by a staff member who is experienced enough to represent your organization in a thoroughly professional manner; (2) they must be conducted according to a carefully structured interview format to be sure that you get the type of feedback you need; and (3) you must allow for probing for additional ideas as the conversation develops.

Exhibit 3 illustrates a sample interview script. The interviewer is conducting research to test the viability of doing a workshop entitled "Evaluating Managerial Performance in Business and Industry." The target group is presidents of medium to large companies.

Exhibit 3. Interview Script for Program Development Ideas.

"Hello, my name is _____ , and I am from [insert the name of your organization]. We are thinking of doing a workshop entitled 'Evaluating Managerial Performance in Business and Industry.' I am calling you to see if I might have a few minutes of your time. I'd like to discuss some program ideas and ask for your reactions. There are two basic purposes for this research: (1) to ascertain whether or not there is a good market for such a program, and (2) to find out what people in a position such as yours would like to see included in such a program. Would you be willing to spend five minutes with me on the phone helping us out with this type of research?"

[Pause to gain approval. If the person seems hesitant, ask if there is a more convenient time when you might call back. Most people, however, will gladly volunteer their time for this type of research. *Hint:* If the person to whom you want to talk has a secretary, you may have to make an appointment with the secretary to talk with the person on the phone in order to get them. Be sure to explain to the secretary what kind of research you are doing and why. Under these conditions, most secretaries will gladly arrange an appointment for you to talk with their boss.]

[After gaining approval for the interview with the person to whom you are speaking, follow a format similar to this:]

"To review, we are thinking of doing a workshop on evaluating managerial performance in business and industry. What kind of initial reactions do you have to this program topic?"

"If you were to attend such a workshop, specifically what kind of important issues would you like to see addressed?"

"If you were to attend, what kinds of questions would you like to get answers to?"

"Could you recommend several top experts in the field whom we might contact to be presenters?"

"What are the main problems you face in evaluating the administrative performance of others in your own organization?"

"What length of time could you or your staff afford to be away from the office in order to attend such a workshop?"

"On a scale of 1 to 4, how likely would you be to attend personally?"

	1	2	3	4
Unsure	Definitely not	Probably not	Probably would	Definitely would

Exhibit 3. Interview Script for Program Development Ideas, Cont'd.

"On the same scale of 1 to 4, how likely would you be to send or encourage a member of your staff to attend?"

	1	2	3	4

Unsure	Definitely not	Probably not	Probably would	Definitely would

"To which people in your organization would you recommend that we send a brochure describing such a program?" [Probe for names as well as titles of positions.]

"What type of benefits would you like to receive from the program if you were to attend?"

"According to what you know about the audience, what would be the best months and dates within a month to attend?"

"If you were to attend, what cities would appeal to you most?"

"What days of the week would be most convenient?"

"Since people in your type of position are very busy and attend many conferences and workshops, what are the major meetings and conventions we should avoid conflicting with in order to attract people like yourself?" [Inquire about dates of those meetings and conventions.]

"What would you be willing to pay to attend an excellent program on this topic?"

"Do you have any additional comments that you think might be helpful as we consider this idea?"

"I really appreciate your time and excellent suggestions. As a result of this research, we will be deciding whether or not to actually go ahead with such a program. If we do proceed, I'd like to send you an advance copy of our brochure so that you can have a sneak preview to see how your responses helped to shape the program."

[*Hint:* Be sure to follow up the telephone interview promptly with a thank-you letter.]

Source: Planning and Marketing Conferences and Workshops: Tips, Tools, and Techniques, by Robert G. Simerly. San Francisco: Jossey-Bass. Copyright ©1990. Permission granted to reproduce.

After completing ten to fifteen interviews, you will have collected much excellent information. In fact, from these responses, you will be in a better position to make decisions about whether or not to go ahead with the program. If you do decide to proceed, their remarks will be useful as you write program copy. Remember to use their terminology because they are speaking in the language of your potential registrants. This will make copy sound true with the reader.

Hint: Be prepared to hear that you may have a bad idea and they will not attend. This too is excellent information. If this is the case, you are better off learning this before you have invested time, energy, and money in an expensive advertising campaign, only to find that you do not attract enough people to break even.

Tip 6
Keep the names and addresses of people you interview using the above script.

Then, if you do offer the program, do the following:

• Send them an advance copy of your brochure in its typewritten form. Thank them again for their help and invite them to register. You might even offer them a special discount because of their valuable assistance.

• When your brochures are printed, write them another letter and enclose ten brochures. Express your thanks and ask them to pass the brochures along to interested colleagues. Be sure to code these so you can track the responses.

When people have spent time helping you brainstorm ideas that actually develop into a program, they have already psychologically begun to be committed to the program. Many program planners who use this technique report that up to 80 percent of the people they interview under these conditions actually convert to program registrations or send a member of their staff.

Tip 7
Send out a call for papers and workshops.

Another useful way to develop a program is to send out a call for papers and workshops before a detailed brochure announcing the actual content of the program is mailed. This is a technique that is particularly useful in academic and other professional circles where the presentation of papers and workshops by participants is an ongoing part of the accepted organizational culture. In order to use this technique, consider the following guidelines:

• Establish a program theme and announce it in the call for papers and workshops.

• The theme should be sufficiently broad to allow as much latitude as possible for encouraging people to submit ideas. At the same time, it should be clearly focused so that respondents will be sure to relate directly to the theme. For example, a call for papers and workshops for educational television professionals listed this theme: "Positioning Educational Television for the Twenty-First Century: Politics, Programming, and Financial Realities." Such a topic provides wide latitude for accepting proposals.

• Send out the call far enough in advance so that your best people, who are often also your busiest professionals, will be encouraged to attend. For example, in the above example for educational television, the call went out in January requesting that proposals for papers and workshops be submitted by April. Those whose proposals were accepted were notified by May to prepare for a two-day conference to be held in December. This type of long-range planning is essential if you require a formal paper to be submitted.

• Consider sending a cover letter with the call for papers and workshops. The actual announcement could be in the form of a brochure, or it could be part of a short cover letter with the typed copy outlining all the information about the program enclosed.

• Make special arrangements to get the best-known people in the field to submit proposals for papers and workshops. Often in order to do this you need to make personal phone calls, followed up by a letter and, perhaps, even another phone call. If you are working with a planning or advisory committee, have members phone the best-known people in the field and encourage them to submit.

• For proposals that are accepted, carefully cultivate and monitor the actual development of the paper or workshop from the time presenters have been notified of acceptance to the time of the program. The dropout rate at this point can be significant if people are not constantly reinforced and progress is not checked.

This idea is an excellent way to develop an entire program. It involves people and it allows the leading experts to help structure the program content. If you accept enough papers and workshops it ensures registrations, and it provides visibility for those participating in the program.

Tip 8
Work with others to develop and cosponsor programs.

Often combining forces with others is an excellent way to develop quality programs. For example, you might cooperate with a state, regional, or national association to cosponsor a program. When this happens, you automatically build in a highly targeted group for marketing, you will be able to access the expertise of the association leadership for an advisory or planning committee, and you will be working with people who usually have a history of what has and has not worked with their programming in the past.

Such groups usually have a wealth of expertise in the content related to their professional field. However, they may need your expertise in marketing and administering the program. This is where you can lend your assistance to help them become more effective. The following guidelines are offered when working with such cosponsorship:

- If they are the content specialists, do not try to take top billing in your advertising. You can achieve equal billing, but you should never try to put the name of your organization ahead of theirs.

- With regard to marketing, keep excellent records of what you have agreed to do and how you plan to measure it afterwards. Groups that enter into cosponsored arrangements often do not attend to these upfront agreements. As a result, if the program does not work out, they will tend to blame the failure on you rather than seeing it as a joint failure.

- Feature the names and titles of advisory and planning committee members prominently in all your advertising. This helps to keep their image prominent, and it helps to legitimize their role as content experts in designing the program.

Many planners of conferences and workshops enter into cosponsorship arrangements each year. In order to be successful in this area, however, it is important that each of you be able to get needs met through cooperation that cannot be met as effectively through solo sponsorship. When this is done, you create a symbiotic relationship that is mutually beneficial to everyone.

Tip 9
Develop slight variations on the same program topic but advertise it to a segmented market.

This is a very effective way to save time, money, and expense on new program development. For example, many people in a wide variety of occupations need to learn how to use electronic spreadsheets for their particular business applications. Therefore, if your program development research indicates that programs on electronic spreadsheets could be ideal for workshops, consider using the general topic but developing different workshops for different segments of the market. For example, here are some possibilities for program topics:

- How to use electronic spreadsheets to maximize profits on the small farm
- How to use electronic spreadsheets for dairy herd management
- How to use electronic spreadsheets to maximize profits in your small business
- How to use electronic spreadsheets to manage money in a continuing education office
- How to use electronic spreadsheets to maximize profits in a law office
- How to use electronic spreadsheets to maximize profits in a medical practice

The list could go on and on. The point is that learning to use electronic spreadsheets is the hot program topic. Therefore, by developing one program on the topic you test the waters for future programs to a different, segmented market. Do not overlook this technique of using the same program idea to apply to a different market. When appropriate, this can greatly enhance your total number of program offerings.

Tip 10
Offer to redesign existing programs to be offered on a special in-house basis.

If you represent an organization that does a wide variety of programs, the chances are good that some of them are appropriate to offer on an in-house basis to meet specific needs of business, industry, government, and education. The types of programs that lend themselves well to an in-house format tend to be those concerned with broad, generic topics. Thus, much of the content can remain the same with slight modifications as you conduct the program in different organizations. Consider these examples:

- A basic leadership course for beginning managers can be redesigned in appropriate ways to be offered on an in-house basis.
- A basic communication skills course lends itself well to in-house adaptation.
- A basic accounting course can be offered in house.
- A course on quality control by statistical methods for engineers can be modified to be appropriate for in-house use in many industrial settings.

The following guidelines are helpful when offering existing courses on an in-house basis:

- Always conduct a thorough needs assessment to determine the demand for the course.
- Do not try to transport the program from one target group to another without any modifications.
- Work with the in-house group to design practical ways in which they can use the material to help solve their everyday problems.

In-house program adaptation is a way to spread the costs of program development over a number of programs. It is also a way to increase revenues at an investment cost that is usually considerably lower than starting from scratch.

Tip 11
Conduct a needs assessment before conducting in-house programs.

Some programs lend themselves well to in-house adaptation without a needs assessment to determine if there is interest in the program. For example, a current update on legal issues related to hiring, evaluation, and termination will often work well with personnel specialists without a needs assessment. This is because the law changes so rapidly in this area that it is often difficult to keep up. Therefore, such a program could be offered once each year in the same organization and still be eagerly received if the material is updated each time. However, before offering most programs, it is important to conduct a needs assessment to ascertain interest and content. Exhibit 4 illustrates a sample form for collecting these data.

Exhibit 4. Needs Assessment for In-House Programs.

The purpose of this survey is to decide what programs we might offer to assist staff in your organization with their professional development. In order to help us serve you better, won't you take a few minutes to respond to the following questionnaire.

1. Please list the five most critical problems you face every day on your job.

    1.

    2.

    3.

    4.

    5.

2. If you were to attend some professional development programs designed to assist you with your everyday management problems, please list topics you would like to see addressed.

    1.

    2.

    3.

    4.

    5.

3. What are the things you like the most about your job?

    1.

    2.

    3.

    4.

    5.

Exhibit 4. Needs Assessment for In-House Programs, Cont'd.

4. If you could make any changes in this organization you wanted in order to help the organization become better, please list what they would be.

    1.

    2.

    3.

    4.

    5.

5. If you could give a friend advice over lunch regarding planning some in-house professional development programs for this organization, what would it be?

6. What do you see as the most pressing problems your colleagues face in the organization?

    1.

    2.

    3.

    4.

    5.

7. Additional remarks:

This short needs assessment will yield data on at least the following issues important to the overall success of the program:

- Identification of real-world, practical problems people face for which a conference or workshop may be the solution
- Identification of issues for which a conference or workshop may not be the best solution
- Identification of things to watch out for as you design the program

This structured needs assessment works equally well in a written format, with individual interviews, or with focus groups.

Tip 12
Increase attendance by giving as many registrants as possible a place on the program.

Many organizations, particularly academic and professional organizations, cannot afford to pay travel and registration fees for staff to attend conferences and professional workshops as participants. However, often organizations will make money available for attendance if their people play a key role in the program.

Therefore, when planning a professional conference, consider issuing a call for papers and workshops as a prelude to announcing the entire program. Almost everyone whose paper or workshop is accepted can be counted on for a confirmed registration. You can also ask people to lead discussion groups, moderate swap shops, and participate in program discussion panels. In this way, they will stand a much greater chance of having all or part of their expenses paid. In addition, you build in success for your program through their participation. Most people who participate in meaningful ways in the program become satisfied with the results. By virtue of their active participation, they become psychologically committed to the program's overall success.

Tip 13
Survey attendees at the current program for advice about future programs.

Your current program attendees are often one of your best sources of ideas regarding new programs. When you explain the purpose of your survey, as well as how filling it out can help you do a better job serving people like them, most people will give careful attention to giving you reliable feedback. For example, Exhibit 5 shows a sample survey that could be given out at a large conference of museum professionals. The format can easily be adapted for use in almost any professional association. The purpose of the survey is to gather information about preferred topics for future conferences and workshops.

Exhibit 5. Program Interest Survey.

As a museum professional, you know how important it is to survey the needs of your market. That is exactly what we are trying to do. We'd appreciate it if you could take a few minutes to respond to the following program interest survey. It will be helpful as we plan our programs for the future.

From the topic areas below, please rate how interested you would be in attending a workshop on each topic.

1. Legal and insurance issues related to collections management

4	3	2	1
Very interested	Interested	Somewhat interested	Not interested

2. How to thrive in spite of recent changes in the tax code related to deductions for gifts to museums

4	3	2	1
Very interested	Interested	Somewhat interested	Not interested

3. Developing personnel policies that avoid legal hassles

4	3	2	1
Very interested	Interested	Somewhat interested	Not interested

4. How to build an effective administrative team in your museum

4	3	2	1
Very interested	Interested	Somewhat interested	Not interested

5. New techniques in conservation

4	3	2	1
Very interested	Interested	Somewhat interested	Not interested

6. How to make your museum more educative

Exhibit 5. Program Interest Survey, Cont'd.

4	3	2	1
Very interested	Interested	Somewhat interested	Not interested

7. Financial management for nonaccountants: how to help museum professionals manage money more effectively

4	3	2	1
Very interested	Interested	Somewhat interested	Not interested

8. How to prepare for accreditation

4	3	2	1
Very interested	Interested	Somewhat interested	Not interested

9. How to conduct an effective capital campaign

4	3	2	1
Very interested	Interested	Somewhat interested	Not interested

10. How to utilize the latest computer software to manage collections

4	3	2	1
Very interested	Interested	Somewhat interested	Not interested

11. Can you suggest three additional topics in which you would be interested?

    1.

    2.

    3.

12. Additional remarks:

This questionnaire allows respondents to indicate their reactions to ten preselected topics. In addition, it gives them a chance to suggest additional topics. Note that in question 11, the survey asks people to suggest three additional topics. Phrasing the question this way usually will prompt respondents to give you more ideas than if you simply ask, "Are there other topics in which you would be interested?" Always ask for a specific number of ideas.

Armed with these data, you are now in a better position to engage in program development for your highest-rated areas. Naturally you will probably want to conduct additional research before proceeding with program development, but this kind of survey separates the hottest topics from the weakest ones.

Hint: You will usually get a much greater response if you hand out the survey during one of your current programs attended by members of your target group. A mail survey is often a second choice because you probably will get a smaller response. However, there are additional advantages to a mail survey. For example, usually you can considerably expand both the number and type of people you reach (lawyers, doctors, and so on).

Tip 14
Design programs to fulfill unmet needs.

One of the main motivators to attend programs is to fulfill unmet needs. We all have them. Therefore, in designing a program, it is very important to determine the unmet needs of your target audience. For example, here are some unmet needs that many program planners find to exist with almost all groups:

- The need to meet and interact with other professionals for the purpose of swapping both information and ideas
- The need to be seen as expert by people back home as a result of attending a program and gaining new skills and knowledge
- The need to get away from my regular job for a short time to refresh myself professionally
- The need to receive public recognition, certificates, or some kind of credit or publicity for participating
- The need to actively find out about the latest ideas in my field
- The need to update myself on the results of current research
- The need to have time away from the job to think through new ideas and ways of solving my daily problems
- The need to get away from the stress of my daily job
- The need just to get out of town and travel for a bit
- The need to become accepted by a larger circle of experts rather than just my own local circle
- The need to document my attendance on my resumé for professional development or job-hunting purposes
- The need to break up my daily routine

This issue of unmet needs being a major motivator for attending conferences and workshops is a complex, multidimensional issue. For example, note that in the above list the unmet needs are almost equally balanced between professional and personal needs. This is a very important concept. People want to attend programs for a wide variety of reasons, both personal and professional. Rarely do people attend for only one reason. Therefore, in order to ensure the best possible success, it is important to plan your program so that it will meet as many of the personal and professional needs of the target audience as possible. Concentrating exclusively on the program content, to the exclusion of more personal needs, is a mistake. Designing a program around only meeting personal needs to the exclusion of substantive content is also a mistake. Excellent programs should help to fulfill both personal and professional needs.

In addition, it is important that brochure copy concretely communicates how people will get these unmet needs met as a result of attending the program.

Tip 15
Plan for a wide variety of learning styles during the course of a program.

Adults do not have a single preferred learning style. Their learning styles vary widely with individuals. For example, here are some of the preferred learning styles people have and how this knowledge can be converted into successful program design:

- *Passive learning style* — Lectures and formal presentations appeal to people having this type of a learning style.
- *Active, concrete learning style* — Simulations, exercises, group discussions, and role playing are usually well received by these people.
- *Scientific experimentation learning style* — Presentation of research results in the form of papers is often popular. These people usually enjoy emphasizing cognitive knowledge.
- *Balanced learning style* — These people often feel equally comfortable with all of the above program approaches.

Naturally, there are many ways to conceptualize people's preferred learning styles. However, the important implication for program design is that audiences are almost always heterogeneous in this regard. Rarely does a group as a whole prefer a single learning style. Therefore, in order to appeal to everyone, it is important to design programs so they contain a combination of approaches to the presentation of content. In this way, you max-imize the chances of creating success and, thus, satisfaction for the entire group.

Tip 16
Build adequate time for socializing into the overall program design.

Most adults like to collaborate and share information about what does and does not work in their occupational roles. They enjoy exchanging tips about the latest ideas in professional practice, hearing others tell stories of successes and failures, and socializing. Therefore, it is important to allow enough time in the program for these activities, since people get important needs met through these social activities.

For example, a provider of workshops for public school administrators, teachers, school board members, and support staff conducted research to find out the main thing that caused people to register for a series of their one-day professional development programs. The advisory committee com-posed of respected leaders in the field felt that it was the program topics and quality of presenters that were the major variables encouraging attendance.

However, personal interviews with a random sample of people attend-ing the workshops revealed startling data that contradicted this firmly held belief. The interviews revealed that the main reason people registered for the programs was that they enjoyed seeing their friends and colleagues dur-ing the coffee breaks and at lunch so they could swap ideas and catch up on the latest news.

As a result, the program planners converted what had been fifteen-minute coffee breaks into half-hour coffee breaks. Lunch time was changed from one hour to one and a half hours. A welcoming continental break-fast was added from 8:00 to 9:00 A.M. when no breakfast had been served before, and a social hour was added from 4:00 to 6:00 after the program was over. As a result of these changes in the program design, attendance increased dramatically, as did satisfaction on the evaluations. The message was clear — program was important, but the social activity was equally im-portant. Therefore, programs and social activities had to be carefully inter-twined as part of the total program design of workshops for this target group.

Tip 17
Establish specific goals for each program.

Well-designed conferences and workshops should have very specific goals. These goals should be established at the beginning of the program planning process so that all content and methods of presentation can be geared to achieving these goals. Then these goals should be communicated clearly to prospective registrants through effective advertising. In addition, these goals need to be clearly communicated to all program presenters as well as staff. In this way, everyone will arrive for the program with the same set of expectations. You will also be able to design evaluations to assess whether or not your established goals were met (Chapter Six offers many tips on how to do this). A guideline for establishing clear program goals is that they should contain an inspirational quality, a sense of urgency, a sense of professional expertise, and a sense of realism.

For example, here are the goals for a one-day program for personnel managers of large businesses. The topic was how to increase minority hiring.

- To provide an update on the legal responsibilities of businesses regarding minority hiring
- To provide case studies of actions of personnel departments in businesses that succeeded in increasing minority hiring
- To examine the social responsibility businesses have to increase minority hiring
- To provide a list of ten articles outlining guidelines to establishing successful minority hiring practices
- To link participants into local, state, regional, and national networks that can assist in finding quality minority applicants to consider for job openings

Note that all of these goals spell out very clearly exactly what will be covered in the content. Thus, by establishing these goals early in the program planning process, it is possible to ensure that all aspects of the program work together in a synergistic way to achieve these goals. Any proposed program session can be measured against these goals to see if it supports goal attainment, and selection of program presenters can be carried out to achieve these goals. Attainment of these goals can be measured during an evaluation at the end of the program.

There is no substitute for establishing clear goals early in the planning process to ensure a successful program.

Tip 18
Survey current magazines and newspapers for program development ideas.

Read. Read. Read. This is an excellent way to scan the environment for new program ideas. For example, here is how one program planner got an idea for a new workshop.

The planner was shopping for new program ideas for financial planners. She began scanning copies of *Money Magazine, Forbes, Business Week, Time, U.S. News & World Report, Newsweek,* and the *New York Times*. As a result of her scanning, reading, and taking notes over a three-month period, she noticed these trends emerging in the popular literature related to financial planning:

- Many financial planners do not necessarily have degrees in finance, economics, banking, accounting, or a field closely related to the business of financial planning.
- As a result of constant changes in the tax laws and the recent interpretations of the law, many financial planners admit privately that it is difficult to keep up to date. Magazine interviews with planners revealed that many of them were frustrated over this.
- Most colleges and universities do not have special academic programs to prepare people to be financial planners.
- The only organization offering accreditation for financial planners is an organization based in Denver that offers correspondence courses that, when successfully completed, lead to accreditation.
- The profession of financial planning is growing so rapidly that it is difficult to get agreement on specific skills, degrees, or educational background that should be required for financial planners.
- Except for two large, national conferences, there are generally not many conferences, institutes, or workshops targeted to financial planners.

As a result of seeing these trends emerge from her reading, the program planner called together an advisory group of financial planners from her community to brainstorm possible program topics for workshops. What emerged were suggestions for the following topics:

- What financial planners need to know about the law in order to avoid being sued
- Update on the latest prepackaged computer software to help develop financial plans for clients
- How changes in last year's tax laws affect financial planning
- How to tell dogs from winners when marketing financial products to clients

Additional testing of these ideas showed that all four topics were worthy of separate program development and could be marketed to the same audience by spreading them over a three-year period. The research indicated that the last topic was even hot enough to warrant a regional, two-day conference. Research also indicated that the other topics were more appropriate for separate, one-day local workshops that could be marketed in seven different cities within the region.

Summary

The tips for program development presented in this chapter have been proven to be successful by a wide array of professionals who plan conferences and workshops. Good program development takes time, and rarely can it be hurried. Ideas need to be developed, and issues need to be researched.

You need to test ideas out on different people and ask for their response. And then you need to let the program roam around in your head for a while so your unconscious as well as conscious thought processes can go to work on it. In this way you can be assured of developing the best possible programs that are consistent with the needs of the market as well as the priorities and values of your organization.

Exhibit 6. Checklist for Program Development.

This checklist is designed to serve as a guide for you to consider so that you include important items in the program planning process. Use it, plus additional items you can add to the list, to ensure that you do not unintentionally overlook any important items.

_____ 1. Clearly distinguish between advisory and planning committees.

_____ 2. Communicate to committee members exactly what is expected of them. Be sure to confirm this in writing.

_____ 3. Begin the first advisory or planning committee meeting with an informal, welcoming activity if possible.

_____ 4. Design appropriate places on the program for some or all of the committee members.

_____ 5. Conduct telephone interviews with potential attendees in order to help structure program content.

_____ 6. Follow up telephone interviews with a thank-you letter.

_____ 7. Keep the names and addresses of people you interview. If an actual program results from your research, send them another letter with an advance, typed copy of the brochure that will be printed.

_____ 8. When the brochures are actually printed, send them a cover letter and ten copies of the brochure, and ask them to distribute the brochures to interested colleagues.

_____ 9. Consider issuing a call for papers and workshop presentations as a way to develop dynamic programs.

_____ 10. When using a call for papers or workshops, be sure that your program theme is sufficiently broad to allow as much latitude as possible for encouraging people to submit ideas.

_____ 11. Actively solicit leaders in the field to submit proposals for papers and workshop presentations.

_____ 12. Carefully cultivate and monitor people who are accepted for papers and workshops. The dropout rate from busy people for this type of format can be high if you do not.

_____ 13. Work with others to develop and cosponsor programs.

_____ 14. Give cosponsors at least equal billing.

_____ 15. When using cosponsorship, keep excellent records of what you have agreed to do and how you plan to measure your success.

_____ 16. Feature the names and titles of advisory and planning committee members prominently in your advertising.

_____ 17. Consider giving as many registrants as possible a place on the program if this is appropriate to your overall program design.

_____ 18. Survey program attendees for advice about new program development.

Exhibit 6. Checklist for Program Development, Cont'd.

_____ 19. Conduct research to determine the unmet needs of your target group.

_____ 20. Design programs to fulfill specific unmet needs.

_____ 21. Plan the program to appeal to a wide variety of learning styles.

_____ 22. Build adequate time for socializing into the overall program design.

_____ 23. For longer programs, plan adequate free time.

_____ 24. Establish specific goals for each program.

_____ 25. Ensure that the program is compatible with the priorities and values of your organization and any cosponsoring organization.

_____ 26. Survey current magazines, periodicals, and newspapers for program development ideas.

Source: Planning and Marketing Conferences and Workshops: Tips, Tools, and Techniques, by Robert G. Simerly. San Francisco: Jossey-Bass. Copyright ©1990. Permission granted to reproduce.

2

Reaching Potential Participants:

Thirty-Four Tips for Mailing List Selection, Maintenance, and Tracking

This chapter is for program planners whose primary means of reaching potential participants is through direct-mail advertising. The tips work equally well for planners of conferences and workshops in the profit or nonprofit sector. One of the most important keys to getting the number of registrants needed to break even is defining the best possible mailing list and mailing enough brochures to attract registrants. This chapter offers a wide variety of tips for increasing your profits through the selection, maintenance, and tracking of mailing lists. The following three guidelines are helpful:

1. Carefully define exactly who is your target audience. This will enable you to compile the type of list to reach your target group.
2. Develop a reliable system to manage your in-house lists. Since past participants form an important part of your in-house list, they are often the best prospects for future registrations.
3. Establish an effective tracking system for all lists so that it is possible to analyze which lists are most effective in actually producing registrants. Developing this kind of in-house data base is essential in helping select the best possible lists for future programs.

Following the above three guidelines will ensure quality control in list selection, management, and tracking. Effective list selection, management, and tracking take time and money so resources must be allocated to this important activity. The following tips illustrate how to achieve success in this area.

Tip 19
Rent mailing lists from large, reliable, well-established professional list houses.

There are hundreds of list houses across the country that specialize in renting mailing lists for direct-mail advertising. For a complete list of names, addresses, and phone numbers of these list houses, consult:

Direct Mail List Rates and Data
Standard Rate and Data Service, Inc.
3004 Glenview Road
Wilmette, IL 60091
Telephone: (312) 256–6067

Pick several of the large, reliable, well-established professional list houses. Interview their salespeople over the phone. Discuss your needs and ask for their recommendations for the direct-mail advertising of your conference or workshop. Compare the advice and prices you get from several list houses before making your choice.

Hint: Establish a continuing relationship with three or four list houses so they can get to know the special needs of your organization and its programs. In this way they will be better able to serve your special list selection needs on a continuing basis.

Tip 20
Use membership lists from professional associations.

As you research your market, you may find that members of certain professional associations are likely targets for your advertising. Consult the following publication:

Encyclopedia of Associations
Gale Research Company
Book Tower
Detroit, MI 48226
Telephone: (313) 961–2242

This classic work is invaluable for compiling mailing lists. It contains the names, addresses, and phone numbers of over 15,000 associations with information about numbers of members, divisions within each association, and information about annual conferences and publications. A few minutes with this encyclopedia will enable you to collect a wealth of information about mailing lists when your target group is a member of one of the over 15,000 associations listed.

Tip 21
Lists obtained from list houses and associations are usually rented, not purchased.

A common misunderstanding is that ordering a list from a professional list house means you are purchasing a list. In reality, lists are rarely purchased. Usually they are only rented, and the terms of the rental agreement are spelled out on the order form. For example, if you order one copy of a list, you are usually renting the list for a one-time use for a specific project. If you order four copies of a list, you are usually renting the list for use for four different mailings. The list, however, normally remains the property of the list house or professional association. It is not yours unless the terms of the contract clearly specify that you are actually purchasing the list and have permission to copy and use it.

Tip 22
Do not make a copy of any rented list.

It is illegal to make a copy of any rented mailing list. Under the conditions of your rental agreement, you may use the list only in the format provided and for the mailing specified on your order. In fact, many list houses and professional associations require that you provide them with copies of your direct-mail advertising before they will send you their lists.

List houses are businesses designed to make a profit. The lists are part of their assets. Therefore, lists are copyrighted and under the terms of the rental agreement you are not allowed to copy the list in *any* format. This includes making a copy on a copy machine or entering the names and addresses into your own computer.

There are serious legal penalties for violating this contractual arrangement with list houses. And in order to encourage people who rent lists to comply with the law in relation to this issue, list houses will often seed their lists with several names and addresses that are dummies. Thus your advertising is sent to an address designed to receive advertising mailed to the addresses on the rented lists maintained by the list house. Staff carefully check all incoming mail and they can usually quickly spot anyone who has made illegal copies of one of their lists.

Tip 23
Consider using list brokers to compile and order your mailing lists.

List brokers are knowledgeable, skilled direct-mail professionals who specialize in compiling and renting mailing lists for clients. Because they do this for a living, they are able to work with you in conceptualizing who you want to reach, selecting the most effective lists for reaching your target groups, and securing the most cost-effective lists suitable for your particular direct-mail advertising needs.

Working with a professional list broker has the following advantages:

- It saves time. They shop for lists for you.
- It saves money. Because of their extensive contacts, they can usually obtain the best lists at the best rates.
- They act as your direct-mail expert consultant and make recommendations on compiling a mailing list based on the individual needs of your particular advertising project.
- They have no allegiance to any single list house or association. Therefore, they will often recommend lists from several different sources as being best for meeting your needs.
- List brokers usually receive a commission of 15 to 20 percent of the cost of the list rental. However, the list house from which the list is rented pays this commission rather than you having to pay it. Thus, using the help of a professional list broker does not cost you any more than doing all of this yourself.

Tip 24
Shop for several list brokers with whom you can build a long-term relationship.

List brokers are professionals, and like all professionals, they can do their best job if they can get to know your organization and its special needs. This takes time. Therefore, shop for several list brokers who are willing to take the time to find out about your organization and its special needs regarding direct-mail advertising.

If you live in a city that has professional list brokers, you can visit them and get to know them personally. If you use out-of-town list brokers, take the time to establish a continuing relationship over the phone. In this way the broker can be aware of your continued needs for lists and the special requirements you have, and thus can give you the best possible professional advice on a continuing basis.

Using professional list brokers will almost always work to your advantage. If you are not already doing so, consider the many advantages you can obtain by relying on this professional free advice.

Tip 25
Remember, a list broker should only provide you with the best possible advice and order your list after *you* have decided which lists are most appropriate.

Do not expect miracles from list brokers. Seek their advice, but in the final analysis the choice of lists is yours. You are in the best position to know the unique requirements of your particular direct-mail advertising project. Never turn over this final choice to anyone else. Following this principle will also encourage you to become an expert on list selection and direct-mail marketing. This, in turn, will make you more valuable to your organization.

Tip 26
Target very specifically exactly whom you want to reach for each mailing.

Whether you are using a list house, a list broker, or your own internal mailing list, it is essential to target very clearly exactly whom you want to reach for any direct-mail advertising. An easy way to do this is to write down a list of the specific job titles of people you want to attract to a particular program and to seek the advice of people holding the job titles you want to reach. They can often suggest additional job titles that you have not thought of. Also ask the advice of staff members and planning committee members. Then, armed with this information, you are in a much better position to discuss your requirements with a list house or a list broker, and to identify the individual segments of your in-house list that you will need.

Tip 27
Consider the Yellow Pages of the phone book as a source for mailing lists.

The Yellow Pages often contain the most up-to-date information regarding names and addresses for business, industry, government, education, and the many trades and professions. There are three basic ways to consider using the Yellow Pages for creating a mailing list:

1. You can input the names and addresses into your own computer and thus create an in-house mailing list. When you do this, however, often you will need to enter only the business name and address and then put in a generic title such as "president" or "manager" for the first line. Naturally, when you send mail to generic titles rather than specific names and addresses, you run the risk that your advertising will never reach your targeted person. For professionals such as physicians, accountants, and attorneys, you can obtain both their names and addresses from the Yellow Pages.

2. You can inquire from the public information office at the phone company how you can go about renting or purchasing their lists.

3. You can work with a list broker to secure these lists.

You could, for example, rent the entire Yellow Pages list or any combination of subsets of the list. Consider this easy-to-obtain source of accurate names and addresses for any city in which you plan to hold a program.

Tip 28
When ordering any list, always check all of the information provided on the data card.

Mailing list houses publish a data card for each list they maintain. This card contains all the essential facts about each list, such as:

- Description of the list
- Source of names and addresses
- Number of people on the list

- Cost of renting the list
- Subsets of the list that can be selected — such as age, income, geographic region, state, county, and zip code
- Format
- Restrictions on use
- Broker policy
- Contact persons

Other inquiries are usually best handled by speaking directly to the sales representative at the list house or by asking your list broker to obtain this information. This additional information includes the following:

- How often is the list updated?
- When was the last time this was done?
- What policies does the list house have regarding NIXIES (undeliverable names because the person has moved or the address is incorrect)? Many list houses offer a guarantee that no more than a certain small percentage of the names will be NIXIES or they will give you a refund.

Tip 29
You can obtain many lists free from many organizations just by asking.

This is particularly true if you have a representative of that organization on an advisory council or planning committee. For example, a representative of a local civic club on a planning committee is usually willing to contribute his or her membership list free of charge. The same is true for officers in corporations, officials in government agencies, members of educational organizations, and members of professional associations.

If they believe in your program and have played a role in helping to plan it, they almost always will have some valuable mailing lists to contribute. Plan to use this source for reliable, free mailing lists.

Tip 30
Ask all presenters at your programs for their mailing lists or a list of their professional acquaintances who might be interested in attending the program.

This can often prove to be one of your best mailing lists. Presenters can provide you with rosters of past participants in their programs. If these participants liked the previous program and yours is sufficiently different, they very likely will be motivated to attend. And follow the never-to-be-violated principle for tracking — code these lists separately by presenter and track responses.

Hint: Even if such a list does not produce many registrants, test it with other, similar programs featuring different presenters. People who have attended one conference or workshop are usually predisposed to attend other, similar programs. By careful testing and tracking, you can determine whether or not they turn out to be hot prospects that need to be cultivated or cool prospects that should be dropped from your internal list.

Tip 31
Conduct a survey as a means of acquiring names for a mailing list.

This technique combines your need to conduct research for program development ideas as well as to collect names for mailing lists. Using this technique, send a written survey to an identified target group asking them to indicate program areas in which they have an interest. Then when they return the survey, also ask for names and addresses of colleagues they think would like to receive information about your upcoming programs.

Hint: This technique tends to work best when the following four conditions are met. First, it works best if you are an established organization that already has name recognition with the public for quality conferences and workshops. Second, it works well if you have an established, loyal clientele. Thus, people will feel that if they refer their friends to you, they are doing them a favor by making it easy to receive information about your upcoming programs that they already know to be credible. Third, the technique is most effective when the survey is only one page long and is accompanied by a cover letter from the most appropriate high-ranking official in your organization. Fourth, the survey should be accompanied by a personal cover letter that has the recipient's name and address typed in as part of the inside address and contains the appropriate personal salutation—such as "Dear Ms. Maxwell." Impersonal form cover letters rarely encourage responses from busy people. Exhibits 7 and 8 provide a sample of cover letters and surveys.

Exhibit 7. Cover Letter to Be Used with Survey.

Dear Ms. Maxwell:

We need your help! We are planning to expand our conferences and work-shops in the near future in order to better serve businesses in our area.

Won't you take three or four minutes to fill out the enclosed short interest survey and return it to us in the stamped, self-addressed envelope? We appreciate your response.

Thanks.

Sincerely,

Robert G. Simerly

P.S. By responding, you can better help us to offer programs targeted to fulfilling the professional development needs of your employees.

[Note that the P.S. is used as a visual way of highlighting to the addressee the benefit she and her organization will receive by responding.]

Source: Planning and Marketing Conferences and Workshops: Tips, Tools, and Techniques, by Robert G. Simerly. San Francisco: Jossey-Bass. Copyright ©1990. Permission granted to reproduce.

Exhibit 8. Program Interest Survey.

We are conducting this short survey in order to better serve the professional development needs of people in our community. Won't you take several minutes to respond and return this survey in the stamped, self-addressed envelope?

Thanks for your assistance.

In what program areas do you have the most need for professional development for your staff? (Check your top four needs.)

____ Time management	____ Strategic planning
____ Communication skills	____ Financial planning
____ Leadership skills	____ Legal issues in personnel
____ Meeting government and	management
regulatory requirements	____ Team building
____ Dealing with difficult	____ Dealing with difficult
clients	employees
____ Basic supervisory skills	____ Using quality circles
____ Advanced supervisory skills	____ International trade

Are there other areas in which you would like to see us develop programs?

Your name_____

Your position_____

Business address_____

_____

_____

          City   State   Zip

Exhibit 8. Program Interest Survey, Cont'd.

Do you know of colleagues who should receive announcements about our upcoming programs? If so, please list their names and addresses here and we will be sure they receive our information.

Thanks for your time. Please return to Wanda Stiller in the enclosed stamped, self-addressed envelope.

Source: Planning and Marketing Conferences and Workshops: Tips, Tools, and Techniques, by Robert G. Simerly. San Francisco: Jossey-Bass. Copyright ©1990. Permission granted to reproduce.

Tip 32
When compiling a large list, consider running a merge/purge to eliminate duplicate names.

Merge/purge is a computer process that eliminates duplicate names and addresses from multiple lists that are compiled for a single mailing. When running a merge/purge, be sure to obtain a price for this service in advance. In this way you can make a decision as to whether a merge/purge is worth the additional money.

If you are renting all lists for a project from the same list house, they can arrange for the merge/purge. If you are renting lists from different houses, a list broker can arrange for a merge/purge. In this case, the data from the list are usually delivered on computer tape to an organization with computer equipment to do the merge/purge. They combine all the data on computer tapes from the various list houses, conduct the merge/purge, and mail you or your list broker the labels in the format requested.

Note: If the merge/purge is too expensive, consider the next tip.

Tip 33
Stagger mailings as an alternative to a merge/purge.

Unless you are dealing with a very large mailing — 50,000 or more — comprising many different mailing lists that have been compiled to reach your target audience, you may find that it is more cost-effective simply to allow the duplicated names to receive more than one copy of your advertising.

However, if this is your decision, stagger the mailing dates so that your recipients will receive duplicate mailings several days apart. When this happens, duplicate mailings received on different days will tend to be viewed in a positive way that reinforces the advertising message. Receiving five copies of an identical brochure on the same day, however, creates a negative, impersonal impression that conveys you are wasting money through indiscriminate mailings. There is a subtle difference here when viewed from the standpoint of the recipient. One creates a positive image that reinforces your advertising message, while the other creates a negative image.

Staggering mailings, of course, involves planning additional lead time in order to allow for these staggered mailing dates. For example, if you have forty-five different lists that you suspect will have some duplicated names, it becomes impractical to do this. However, you could stagger the mailings and do them in five segments spread out over fifteen days.

Tip 34
Carefully consider the format in which you wish to receive your mailing lists.

Cheshire and Avery labels are the most common label formats for most providers of conferences and workshops. Cheshire labels are printed on computer paper, usually in a three-up or four-up format. This means that there will be three or four rows of labels across the paper. Cheshire labels are designed to be used by mailing houses that have special machines to affix glue to the label, cut it, and affix it to the advertising piece. Avery labels are peel-off labels that need to be affixed by hand.

Another way to receive data for labels is to order computer tape. You then generate the labels on your own equipment, or a mailing house uses its equipment to generate labels. This is the format you will need if you wish to have the name and address printed directly on the envelope or mailing label of the advertising.

With the sophistication of today's computer software and hardware, it is even possible to print a name and address on an envelope so that it simulates the appearance of a hand-addressed letter. Generally, this process is only used for very large mailings of over 75,000 names.

Providers of all but the largest conventions, meetings, conferences, and workshops usually find the Cheshire or Avery format to be more cost-effective. For example, a high-speed machine can affix over 30,000 Cheshire labels in about an hour.

Tip 35
Determine the most cost-effective format for ordering labels.

The format in which you order labels will determine the cost for affixing them. For example, if you are using a mailing house for this process, you will usually find that ordering Cheshire labels is more cost-effective for any mailing of over 1,000 pieces. Since Avery labels must be attached by hand, costs for this hand labeling will be added to your bill. To determine the break point in price for Cheshire versus Avery labels, contact your mailing house. They can provide you with accurate guidelines designed to save you money.

And remember, if you use Avery labels and have your own staff affix them, you still have costs for staff time. Most providers of conferences and workshops find that it is almost always more cost-effective to have a professional mailing house handle all labeling for them for any project over 1,000 items.

Tip 36
Locate a reputable mailing house and develop an ongoing relationship with them.

There are three good ways to locate someone who will handle your mailings for you.

1. Consult your Yellow Pages.
2. Consult the *Direct Mail List Rates and Data* publication of Standard Rate and Data.
3. Inquire of your printer. In fact, many large printers now provide this service themselves. If not, they usually know who the most reliable mailing houses are that are convenient to you.

Tip 37
When ordering lists, always request the nine-digit zip code rather than just the five-digit zip code.

Because the nine-digit zip code helps the post office speed up the delivery of mail, it is to your advantage to use it. The lists cost the same when rented from a list house, and the post office gives a price break on postage when the nine-digit zip is used. Therefore, using it not only speeds up delivery but it also saves you money.

Tip 38
Always order labels separated by zip codes.

Doing this will save you money in handling charges for all mailings done at bulk rates. Only first-class mail is accepted by the post office without being sorted and bundled by zip code. Thus, ordering your labels already separated by zip codes saves handling money. When this is done, it is simply a matter of you or your mailing house identifying the beginning and ending of each zip code and bundling the advertising into separate bundles to be delivered to the post office.

Tip 39
When using mailing lists, remember that from 15 to 30 percent of the population changes its address each year.

Because of our highly mobile population, accurate mailing lists have a very short life. When maintaining your own list, be sure to update it at least every two years. When renting lists from list houses, find out when the list was last updated and the criteria and methods used for updating. If it is over two years old, seriously question whether or not to use it. Remember, if someone is trying to rent or sell you an old list, you can almost always get a more reliable, recent list at the same price.

Tip 40
Create a simple way to update your internal mailing list.

Internal lists have a tendency to grow at exponential rates. They also have a tendency not to get updated often because this takes time and money. If up to 30 percent of the population changes its address each year, depending on the city, within two years your internal list could be out of date because half of the people on the list may have moved. Therefore, at least every two years you should update your internal lists.

An easy way to do this is to mail a stamped, self-addressed postcard that allows people to respond if they wish to continue receiving your literature. Exhibit 9 shows a sample of copy that can be printed on a self-mailing card.

Hint: If you do telemarketing for programs, obtain the person's phone number. Otherwise this can be omitted.

Exhibit 9. Card for Updating Internal Mailing Lists.

[Prominently display the name and address of your organization and any other pertinent information at the top of the card so that people can easily see who is requesting a response. People are much more likely to respond if they instantly recognize your organization.]

Periodically we update our mailing lists in order to serve you better. Won't you take a few moments to fill out and return this card? We appreciate your help.

_____ Please keep me on your mailing list. My name and address as shown on the mailing label are correct.

_____ Please remove me from your mailing list.

_____ Please note my change of address below.

Name_____

Position title_____

Name of business_____

Address_____

_____

	City	State	Zip

Phone_____

Area code   Number

Are there colleagues or friends you can recommend who should receive our literature? If so, just list their names and addresses and we will be sure that they receive announcements of upcoming programs.

_____

_____

_____

_____

_____

_____

_____

[The front of the postcard is stamped and addressed to you.]

Source: Planning and Marketing Conferences and Workshops: Tips, Tools, and Techniques, by Robert G. Simerly. San Francisco: Jossey-Bass. Copyright ©1990. Permission granted to reproduce.

Tip 41
When updating your lists, be careful not to mail out a request for updating that will allow people to delete themselves from your preferred list.

Sometimes it is important to mail to people who are not necessarily good candidates for registering for programs simply because you want them to continue receiving your information. This helps establish your presence and image in the marketplace. For example, a very large museum that maintained an internal list of 20,000 names had a subsection dubbed its preferred list. This list of 500 people was composed of key influentials in the community — members of city government, presidents of large businesses, identified patrons of the arts and humanities, and people who took first-class travel/study tours to English estates and other historical sites abroad sponsored by the museum.

The museum determined that they wanted these 500 influential opinion makers to know about all of their upcoming programs. Therefore, they maintained them as a preferred list. Updating this list consisted of personally monitoring any change of address rather than mailing them a card asking whether or not they wished to remain on the mailing list. Thus, the main purpose of having them on the preferred list was not to gain registrations for programs but rather to constantly keep them informed about a wide variety of museum activities and thus keep the image of the museum and its programs in their minds.

Tip 42
When renting outside lists or using your own internal mailing lists, code each list so that the effectiveness of that list in drawing registrants can be tracked.

Track all mailing lists to build a data base for determining which lists draw best for you. When using your own internal lists, be sure that the computer software for creating and maintaining the list has the ability to print a code of your choice in a corner of the mailing label. When renting outside lists, instruct the list provider to code each list separately with the code you provide. This code usually appears in the upper right-hand corner of the label. All list houses and list brokers have provisions for doing this.

One of the most often made mistakes in direct-mail marketing is failure to code and track the responses for every mailing list — without exception. It is only through this coding, tracking, and subsequent analysis that you can determine the cost-benefit for using various lists, whether they are your own internal lists or external lists.

Tip 43
Be sure that a large list has appropriate subcategories and that these categories are coded separately for tracking.

A large list obtained from a list house or other source is almost always composed of subsets of smaller lists. Coding only the large list with a single code does not necessarily provide the kind of information valuable in your marketing analysis. For example, a meeting provider organized a seminar entitled "Time Management for the Busy Executive." It mailed 75,000 brochures to a list described by the list house as consisting of the leading business people in Los Angeles. The entire list of 75,000 was coded with the same code.

Even though the mailing did produce the required registrants to break even, an analysis after the fact could not be done to determine which subsets of the 75,000-name list were most effective in producing the largest number of registrants. Actually the list house compiled the list from thirty-seven different sublists of business people. If each of these sublists had been coded separately, they probably would have found that certain lists produced many more registrants than others.

Thus, when having a broker or list house compile a large list, always ask them for a breakdown of the component parts of the compiled list. Then ask that each of these sublists be coded differently. The extra time and effort this takes will reward you with a much more useful analysis of the effectiveness of your various lists in producing registrants for a program. Then for future programs you may find that you can get the same numbers of registrants by eliminating some of the nonproductive subsets on the larger list. This will save you money. For example, one large meeting provider was able to reduce its total marketing expenses by 7.5 percent over a four-year period by becoming more accurate and effective in its tracking efforts.

Tip 44
If you are mailing a brochure not enclosed in an envelope, use the tracking method described here.

Order each list so that a tracking code is printed in the upper right-hand corner of the label. Then print the registration form on the back cover of the brochure directly above the mailing label space. Have your graphic artist draw a bold line around the registration form and the mailing label space so visually they become one unit. Thus, because the registration form and the mailing label are within a bold box, it visually communicates to the respondent not to return the registration form without the mailing label. In addition, even if people return a photocopy to avoid cutting up the brochure, the code will also be returned. This will not be the case if the registration form is on the last page of copy before the back cover. Third, if people register by FAX, it still preserves the mailing label code. Exhibit 10 shows how to do this.

Exhibit 10. Registration/Mailing Label Form.

How to Sharpen Your Business Writing Skills
9 a.m. to 4 p.m.
all locations

May 9, 19__
Double Tree Inn
Seattle, Washington

May 17, 19__
Queen Anne Hotel
San Francisco, California

June 6, 19__
Palmer House
Chicago, Illinois

June 20, 19__
Hotel Majestic
St. Louis, Missouri

*The mission of the University of Nebraska Division of Continuing Studies
is to extend the resources of the university to promote lifelong learning.*

- -

REGISTRATION FORM: Please feel free to duplicate this form for additional registrations if necessary.

FAST, EASY REGISTRATION

BY PHONE
Call us now at:
(402) 472-2175
Please have your address label
and program number ready.
Office hours: Monday–Friday,
8 a.m. – 5 p.m. CST.

BY MAIL
*Mail the entire back cover
with mailing label to:*
**Division of Continuing Studies
Registration and Records
271 Nebraska Center
University of Nebraska–Lincoln
Lincoln, NE 68583-0900**

(If less than 10 working days
before the program, please
register by phone.)

BY FAX
*Fax the entire back cover
with mailing label to:*
(402) 472-1901
Our FAX line is open 24 hours.

Route to:

_____
_____
_____
_____

UNL is a nondiscriminatory institution.

Check the session you plan to attend:

May 9, in Seattle, Washington	_____PDS-053N-022-891Y
May 17, in San Francisco, California	_____PDS-054N-022-891Y
June 6, in Chicago, Illinois	_____PDS-055N-022-891Y
June 20, in St. Louis, Missouri	_____PDS-056N-022-891Y

ORGANIZATION _____

Address _____

_____

City _____

State _____ ZIP _____

Phone Number ( )_____

NAME #1_____
    Last   First   MI

Position _____

Social Security Number _____

NAME #2_____
    Last   First   MI

Position _____

Social Security Number _____

General Registration Fee **$69 each.**
Total payment of _____

METHOD OF PAYMENT

Check (payable to the University of Nebraska) _____

Bill my organization _____
(Attach purchase order or signed authorization)

Charge to:

_____ VISA _____ MasterCard _____ American Express

Card Number _____

Expiration Date _____

Name on card if not registrant _____

Signature _____

Division of Continuing Studies
271 Nebraska Center
University of Nebraska–Lincoln
Lincoln, NE 68583-0900

Nonprofit Org.
U.S. Postage
PAID
Lincoln, NE
Permit No. 46

Source: Planning and Marketing Conferences and Workshops: Tips, Tools, and Techniques, by Robert G.
Simerly. San Francisco: Jossey-Bass. Copyright ©1990. Permission granted to reproduce.

Tip 45
If you cannot print the registration form on the back cover, you can still create a reliable process to track your mailing lists.

While printing the registration form on the back cover of a brochure and requesting registrants to return the form and the mailing label is the most foolproof method of tracking mailing list codes, sometimes this is not possible. For example, for a registration process at a large conference where you offer people many options, sometimes there is not enough room on the back cover to include the registration form.

In cases such as these, print the registration form on the last page before the back cover. Include specific instructions to capture the mailing list code in a large box labeled "Important: Mailing Label Code." Ask the registrants to copy the priority code from the label and insert it in the proper space provided in the box. Exhibit 11 shows how to do this.

Exhibit 11. Registration Form with Priority Code Request.

Executive Development Series Registration Form

Please duplicate as necessary.

The mission of the Division of Continuing Studies is to extend the resources of the university to promote lifelong learning.

Name: _____
Last   First   MI

Social Security Number: _____

Name of Organization: _____

Position: _____

Address: _____

_____

City: _____ State: _____ ZIP: _____

Daytime Phone: (_____) _____

Evening Phone: (_____) _____

Home Address: _____

City: _____ State: _____ ZIP: _____

> **IMPORTANT: MAILING LABEL CODE**
> Fill in the code number as it appears on the mailing label (even if the brochure was addressed to someone other than the participant).
>
> _____

Method of payment

☐ Payment enclosed
    (Make check payable to University of Nebraska)

☐ Bill my organization
    (Attach purchase order or authorization with appropriate signature.)

☐ VISA   ☐ MasterCard   ☐ American Express

Charge card number _____

Expiration date _____

Signature _____

Name on card if other than registrant's _____

Course information

Please indicate which course(s) you are registering for:

Course Title	Instructor	Number	Fee
☐ Managing the Exploding Service Sector	Luthans/Miller	PDS-116N	_____
☐ Communication Techniques for the Executive	Ganster	PDS-117N	_____
☐ Intrapreneurship for Productivity Improvement	Lee/Luthans	PDS-118N	_____
☐ Financial Management and Analysis	Broman	PDS-119N	_____
☐ Strategic Market Planning	Marquardt	PDS-120N	_____

On-site locations

Please indicate at which location you will be attending:

☐ Grand Island   440
☐ Lincoln   300
☐ Norfolk   490
☐ Nebraska CorpNet Locations

CorpNet location

Please check the site where you will be attending:

☐ AT&T	310
☐ Control Data	311
☐ Data Documents	312
☐ 1st National Bank-Omaha	313
☐ Northwestern Bell	314
☐ OPPD	315
☐ 3M	316
☐ Union Pacific	317
☐ Blue Cross/Blue Shield	318
☐ Department of Roads	330
☐ Dorsey Labs	331
☐ Harris Technologies	332
☐ LT&T	333
☐ FirsTier-Lincoln	334
☐ Bryan Hospital	335
☐ St. Elizabeth Hospital	336
☐ Scottsbluff	350
☐ Other _____	

Source: Planning and Marketing Conferences and Workshops: Tips, Tools, and Techniques, by Robert G. Simerly. San Francisco: Jossey-Bass. Copyright ©1990. Permission granted to reproduce.

This method is generally not as effective for tracking as the first method because the respondent must copy the code from the mailing label. However, many respondents will do this. Thus, you will generally be able to capture up to 75 percent of these codes for tracking and analysis.

Most direct-mail professionals find that the key to using this system is to be sure that the mailing code request box is bold, has graphic emblems to attract attention, and has short, clear instructions.

Tip 46
If your advertising plan calls for a direct-mail piece to be enclosed in an envelope, you can still track responses by printing different codes on the registration forms to match the codes on the mailing labels of the envelope.

This takes a little extra time at the printing and mailing stage, but it ensures that you still maintain an effective tracking system. For example, suppose that you have ten different mailing lists for a project. Code the mailing labels for each list differently. List 1 could be coded with an *A* printed on the label, list 2 could have a *B* on the label, and so on. Then have your graphic designer create the registration form to be enclosed in an envelope so that the printer can stop the print run ten times and insert the appropriate codes that match the label codes on the registration form.

When this system is used, it is essential to give the person who coordinates your mailing very specific instructions regarding the importance of matching the correctly coded registration forms to the appropriate mailing label code. Thus, you will ensure that you have maintained an effective tracking system even if your direct-mail piece is enclosed in an envelope.

Tip 47
When accepting phone registrations, be sure to ask the caller for the mailing label code.

Since many providers of conferences and workshops find that over 50 percent of their registrations are by phone, be sure to create a system to capture the mailing label code for phone registrations. The key to making this work is to train phone registration staff how to do this. This should include a comprehensive explanation on why capturing this mailing code is so important. Thus you will be able to track phone registrations as effectively as mail-in registrations.

Tip 48
Make special arrangements for tracking the response to newspaper and magazine ads.

Because newspaper or magazine advertising is so expensive, such ads usually do not actually ask for a registration. Program planners generally use newspaper or magazine ads only to generate inquiries. Here are some important principles to follow for tracking these responses:

- If the ad has a response coupon, code the coupon so you can track responses.
- In addition, if you run more than one ad in the same newspaper or magazine on different dates, code response coupons differently so you can determine which date drew the most respondents.
- For telephone inquiries, you can use two methods for tracking. If you expect a large number of calls in response to an ad, consider installing a special phone line with its own number. Then you can count the calls that come in on that number. As an alternative, you can simply ask callers where they heard about the program. Then record their responses in such a way that you can track them back to individual ads.
- For phone inquiries, be sure to ask callers when they saw the ad. People responding to newspaper ads can usually do this accurately. For magazine ads, you will tend to get less reliable data. For example, many callers will respond, "It was in the last issue of such-and-such magazine."

Tip 49
Create a cost-benefit spreadsheet to analyze the cost-effectiveness for each mailing list for producing actual program registrations.

If you run programs where you do not have to pay for mailing lists, it is sometimes enough just to know how many people each list attracted to register. This information can be tabulated. However, most meeting planners need a more sophisticated system for determining the cost-benefit of each mailing list. Exhibit 12 shows how to do this.

Exhibit 12. Spreadsheet for Cost-Benefit Tracking of Direct-Mail Marketing Activities.

Program Title: Dealing with Upset Citizens
Program Date: October 3
Program Location: Baltimore

List Name _1_	List Code _2_	Number on List _3_	Number Printed _4_	Number of Paid Registrants _5_	Gross Registration Fee Income _6_	% of Total Registration Fees _7_	Registrations per 1,000 Mailed _8_	List/Ad Cost _9_	Postage/ Handling/ Label Cost _10_	Printing, Typesetting, Design, Editing, & Other Costs _11_	Total Marketing Costs _12_	Return on Marketing Investment (6–12) _13_
CEOs in Baltimore	2	8,254	8,785	52	$7,800	16.88%	6	$675.00	$3,237.22	$4,868.83	$8,781.05	($981.05)
Preferred List	3	125	133	3	$450	0.97%	24	$0.00	$49.03	$73.73	$122.76	$327.24
Yellow Pages Presidents	4	6,481	6,898	112	$16,800	36.36%	17	$487.00	$2,541.85	$3,822.98	$6,851.83	$9,948.17
Training Directors	6	568	605	25	$3,750	8.12%	44	$75.00	$222.77	$335.05	$632.82	$3,117.18
Social Service Agency	8	2,359	2,511	10	$1,500	3.25%	4	$195.00	$925.20	$1,391.52	$2,511.72	($1,011.72)
Government Offices	10	2,651	2,822	19	$2,850	6.17%	7	$195.00	$1,039.72	$1,563.76	$2,798.48	$51.52
Past Attendees	11	50	53	5	$750	1.62%	100	$0.00	$19.61	$29.49	$49.10	$700.90
Education	12	3,000	3,294	82	$12,300	26.62%	27	$300.00	$1,176.60	$1,769.63	$3,246.23	$9,053.77
TOTAL		23,488	25,101	308	$46,200	100.00%	13	$1,927.00	$9,302.00	$13,854.99	$24,993.99	$21,205.11

Enter Total Printed: 25,101   Total Income: $46,200

Total Postage, Handling, Labeling Cost: $9,302

Detail of Printing, Typesetting, Graphic Design, Editorial, and Other Costs

Total Printing Costs	$12,560
Total Typesetting Costs	$500
Total Graphic Design Costs	$395
Total Editorial Costs	$200
Other Costs	$75
Photos	$125
TOTAL PRODUCTION COSTS	$13,855

Note: The prototype for this spreadsheet was developed by Dennis Prisk. See Prisk, D. P., "Budgeting for Marketing Activities and Staff Costs," in *Handbook of Marketing for Continuing Education,* Robert G. Simerly and Associates. San Francisco: Jossey-Bass, 1989. Mark Dresselhaus, director of business operations in the Division of Continuing Studies at the University of Nebraska, Lincoln, has modified and adapted the Prisk worksheet.

Source: Planning and Marketing Conferences and Workshops: Tips, Tools, and Techniques, by Robert G. Simerly. San Francisco: Jossey-Bass, ©1990. Permission granted to reproduce.

In column 1 the name of each list is recorded. Column 2 captures the code that is written on each mailing label. Column 3 tracks the total number of names on each list. Column 4 prorates the number printed to each mailing label. This figure of 25,101 is entered at the bottom of column 4, and the spreadsheet is programmed to prorate this number. Column 5 records the actual number of people who registered from each list. By filling in the total income figure at the bottom of column 6, the spreadsheet prorates this to each list. Column 7 records the percentage of registrations netted by each different mailing list. Column 8 identifies the number of registrations per 1,000 brochures mailed. The cost for the mailing labels is recorded in column 9. Postage, handling, and labeling costs are recorded in column 10. By recording the total amount of $9,302 at the bottom of column 10, the spreadsheet prorates the correct amount to each list. By entering the individual costs for printing, typesetting, graphic design, editorial, and other costs, the spreadsheet calculates this to total $13,854.99. The spreadsheet then automatically prorates this cost to each list. Column 12 summarizes total marketing costs and prorates them to each list. These costs are calculated as the sum of $9,302 (postage, handling, labeling), $1,927 (list cost), and $13,854.99 (total production costs), which equals $25,084. Column 13 calculates the return on market investment for each list.

Thus, by developing this sophisticated spreadsheet to assist in a cost-benefit analysis of marketing activities, it is possible to do a better job at developing comprehensive direct-mail marketing plans for future programs.

Tip 50
Seed each list with your name and address or that of one of your staff members so you can track when mail is actually delivered.

This is particularly important if someone other than your office is in charge of labeling, sorting, bundling, and dropping your entire project in the mail. There have been cases of mailing houses or post offices forgetting to complete a mailing or actually discarding it. If you seed each list with your name and address, you can easily track to be sure that each list actually was mailed out.

When doing this, it is important to have your name and address inserted into the computer-printed list rather than typing it or handwriting it at the bottom. In this way, people preparing the mailing will not be aware of this internal check. All list houses have the ability to add your name and address to each list before it is coded, printed, and shipped to you. Ask them to do this. For your internal lists, you can add your seeded names and addresses to the list before you get a computer printout of labels.

Tip 51
When mailing outside your community, seed and track lists to determine the average time it takes for bulk mail to be delivered.

The advantage of using bulk mail is that it enables you to achieve large savings on postage. The disadvantage is that bulk mail has the lowest priority for delivery at each post office through which it passes. Therefore, in order to time mailings that will go outside your local area, seed lists with names and addresses of friends in order to build a data base that will allow you to make reliable estimates of the amount of time it takes for your bulk mail to move across country.

For example, this is the rule of thumb that a number of large providers of conferences and workshops use:

- Local bulk mail — one week for delivery
- Bulk mail within the same state — one to two weeks for delivery
- Bulk mail within the same region — two weeks for delivery
- Bulk mail outside your region — three to four weeks for delivery

A good way to build a reliable data base for determining the average time it takes your mail to be delivered is to seed lists with names and addresses of friends across the country and ask them to notify you what date they received your advertising. Then by matching this against the date the advertising was mailed, it is possible to determine for yourself how much time you need to build into your direct-mail marketing strategy for delivery. Do this for several separate mailings at different times of the year to build a reliable data base for planning your estimates for future mailings.

Tip 52
Capture the names and addresses of everyone who phones in for information about any of your programs.

People who phone in for information about programs are often your best prospects for attending future programs. By virtue of initiating the phone call they have already indicated their interest in your organization and its programs. A mistake often made in marketing is not creating a process to capture these names and addresses to be placed on your internal mailing list. Code these names differently from others, and include a code to indicate they are telephone inquiries. In addition, code them for content area about which they inquired as well as by occupation. This will make it easy to track these lists over time. Exhibit 13 shows a sample call recording slip that can be used by registration staff who handle phone calls from people requesting information about programs.

Exhibit 13. Phone Call Recording Slip.

Use this slip to record data from everyone who phones in to request information about programs.

Date_____

Name_____
Position title_____
Name of business_____
Address_____

_____

| City | State | Zip |

Phone_____
                Area code   Number

Program(s) for which information is requested:

_____

_____

What kind of business or service do they provide?

_____

How did they hear about us?

_____

Additional remarks:

_____

List code (to be filled in by mailing list manager)

_____

Source: Planning and Marketing Conferences and Workshops: Tips, Tools, and Techniques, by Robert G. Simerly. San Francisco: Jossey-Bass. Copyright ©1990. Permission granted to reproduce.

Summary

Mailing list selection, maintenance, and tracking is both an art and a science. It takes time and money in order to achieve excellence in this area so the allocation of these resources must be planned for. Giving careful attention to this important aspect of direct-mail marketing will reward you with more registrants and reduce your marketing costs in relation to income generated. By targeting your audience more effectively and tracking their responses, you can greatly enhance all of your marketing efforts.

Exhibit 14. Checklist for Mailing List Selection, Maintenance, and Tracking.

The following checklist summarizes the major items to include in an effective system for mailing list selection, maintenance, and tracking. Review and modify this list to meet the specific needs of your organization. Then it can form the basis for an effective, ongoing check system.

List Rental Issues

_____ 1. Have lists been rented from a reliable list source such as a professional list house?

_____ 2. Have you secured mailing lists from professional associations as appropriate?

_____ 3. Have you avoided making unauthorized copies of lists?

_____ 4. Have you employed the services of a professional, reliable list broker as appropriate?

_____ 5. Have you considered renting lists from the Yellow Pages of the phone directory?

_____ 6. Have you checked the data card for each list to ensure that the list meets your specific needs?

Acquiring Additional Lists

_____ 7. Have you used reliable sources to obtain appropriate free lists, such as local civic and business clubs?

_____ 8. Have you considered conducting a survey as a means of acquiring mailing lists?

Merge/Purge Issues

_____ 9. Have you considered running a merge/purge for large mailings?

_____ 10. If you do not run a merge/purge, have you arranged to stagger mailings on different days to avoid having recipients receive more than one copy of a brochure on the same day?

Mailing List Format

_____ 11. Have you chosen Cheshire or Avery labels as appropriate for the needs of your mailing?

_____ 12. Have you ordered all labels with the nine-digit zip code rather than just the five-digit zip code?

_____ 13. Have you ordered all labels separated by zip code?

Maintaining Mailing Lists

_____ 14. Have you created a simple way to update all your internal mailing lists?

Exhibit 14. Checklist for Mailing List Selection, Maintenance, and Tracking, Cont'd.

_____ 15. Have you created an internal, preferred mailing list of important opinion makers who need to receive your mailings even if they are not necessarily candidates to attend a program themselves?

Coding and Tracking Mailing Lists

_____ 16. Have you ordered all rented lists with a code on each label for effective tracking?

_____ 17. Do large lists have appropriate subcategories with separate tracking codes?

_____ 18. Is the registration form designed to capture the mailing list code for each registrant regardless of where the registration form appears in your advertising?

_____ 19. Have you designed an effective system for securing the mailing list code for all phone registrations?

_____ 20. Have you designed a special tracking system to track the mail and phone responses for all newspaper and magazine ads?

_____ 21. Have you designed a spreadsheet on a personal computer to help analyze the cost-benefit for your marketing activities for individual programs?

_____ 22. Have you developed a system to capture the names and addresses of everyone who phones in for information about any program?

Source: Planning and Marketing Conferences and Workshops: Tips, Tools, and Techniques, by Robert G. Simerly. San Francisco: Jossey-Bass. Copyright ©1990. Permission granted to reproduce.

3

Establishing
a Quality Image:

Thirty-One Tips for
Graphic Design,
Typesetting, and Printing

Planning for the effective use of graphic design, typesetting, and printing is an important part of marketing. Effectively used, these elements work in positive ways to enhance an organization's image. When used ineffectively, they create negative impressions of your organization and its programs.

Investments in quality graphic design, typesetting, and printing represent some of your best marketing investments. This chapter is devoted to practical tips that you can begin implementing today in order to achieve success in these three areas.

Tip 53
For professional-looking advertising, always employ the services of a first-rate graphic designer.

Graphic designers specialize in translating your communication into graphic form so that readers will be receptive to your message. They are experienced at designing artwork, working with photographers, utilizing type styles and size to communicate effectively, and working with printers in selecting the right kind of paper and color of ink to make your marketing message as effective as possible.

Graphic designers typically have two ways of charging for their services: an hourly rate or a flat rate for the entire job. The latter is the type of billing preferred by most people because it establishes a fixed figure that can be planned for in the overall program budget. When this payment method is used, there will be no surprises at the end of a project.

Tip 54
Secure a letter of agreement from your graphic designer with a price quote for the entire project before proceeding.

In order to avoid any misunderstanding regarding services to be performed, ask your graphic designer for a letter of agreement that spells out all services for a project and lists the total price. While many graphic designers do not go to the trouble of writing out a formal contract, they usually will write out on their letterhead all the services they will charge for a project along with all charges. This then becomes a contract. If you as a client request additional services during the course of the project, expect to pay extra for them. When this is necessary, your designer can quote you the price for additional services so you can determine whether or not you want them. Exhibit 15 shows a sample letter of agreement that can be modified to include the specific requirements for each of your projects. This letter of agreement usually originates with the graphic designer after preliminary discussions with the client. Whether you originate the agreement letter or whether it originates with the graphic designer, it is important to address the issues included in the sample in Exhibit 15.

Exhibit 15. Letter of Agreement from a Graphic Designer.

Designs Unlimited

Suite 614   Telephone: (503) 973–1805
127 White Street   FAX: (503) 847–2837
Portland, Oregon

Date:

To: Mary Watkins, Program Director
The Institute of Income Tax Preparers
Suite 125, 3847 Oak Street
Portland, Oregon

From: Jim Trask, Graphic Designer

I am pleased to confirm with you our services to design an 8½-by-11-inch, four-page direct-mail brochure for your conference entitled "How to Save Your Clients Money at Tax Time: A Practical Workshop for Tax Preparation Professionals."

The services we have agreed that we will provide in producing your direct-mail brochure for this program are as follows:

1. When your final brochure copy is finished, we will meet to review the overall concept for your brochure. We will then produce three rough sketches. After we have discussed these, we will modify one of these sketches for you for final approval before proceeding to typesetting.
2. When you have okayed the final sketch, we will mark the copy and deliver it, along with the computer disk of copy you will provide, to the typesetter. (Typesetting will be itemized separately on our bill to you and will depend on actual costs for initial typesetting plus any revisions requested by you other than to correct typesetting errors.)
3. When galleys are returned from the typesetter, you will proof and correct any typographical errors. *Please note that all proofreading and corrections of errors are your responsibility.*
4. You will return the corrected galleys to me, and we will work with the typesetters to make all corrections you have marked.
5. When the corrections have been made, we will proceed to a paste-up designed to give you camera-ready copy according to the final sketch you have approved.
6. We will then ask you to proof and okay this final paste-up by signing your initials on each board. This is your indication that you have made all corrections and that all copy is correct. *It is important to note at this phase that any errors in wording or spelling after you have initialed the boards are your responsibility.*

Exhibit 15. Letter of Agreement from a Graphic Designer, Cont'd.

7.   We will work with you to select the type and color of paper for print-ing. You will approve these selections.

8.   We will also work with you to select the colors of ink to be used. You will also approve these selections.

9.   It will be our responsibility to secure any photographs or design any artwork used in this project. The cost for photographs will be itemized separately on our bill to you and will have been okayed by you prior to taking the photographs. The cost for any artwork produced by our firm is included in the overall price quote.

10. We will provide you with camera-ready boards that you will deliver to the printers.

11. We will check a blueline prior to printing for any mechanical errors that may have occurred at the printers after we have given them our camera-ready boards. You will also be asked to check this blueline when we have finished. Your initials on each page of the final blueline will be your permission to proceed to the final printing.

Our agency fee for the above services will be $500. The price for any additional services you request as the project proceeds will be agreed to before the service is performed, and the final bill will be adjusted accordingly.

Our signatures indicate that we both agree to these terms.

Jim Trask   Date   Mary Watkins   Date

Source: Planning and Marketing Conferences and Workshops: Tips, Tools, and Techniques, by Robert G. Simerly. San Francisco: Jossey-Bass. Copyright ©1990. Permission granted to reproduce.

Tip 55
Know your audience and create graphic design appropriate to them.

Direct-mail advertising must attract the attention of the recipients during the first three to five seconds if it is to be read instead of being discarded. Therefore, it is essential to create a design that will gain instant attention and credibility. Here are some frequently made mistakes for you to avoid:

1. Avoid avant-garde designs for conservative, traditional audiences.
2. Avoid conservative, traditional designs for avant-garde audiences.
3. Blank space, or white space, as it is often called, should be planned for deliberate effect. It should not look like you have white space because you did not have enough copy to fill the page. Have a detailed discussion related to this issue with your graphic designer. Be aware of this when writing copy.
4. Graphic design for your direct-mail advertising should be geared to gaining a definite response — usually a registration for a program. Sometimes this may be at odds with the esthetic layout preferred by a graphic designer who does not have specialized training in direct-mail response. Therefore, it is essential that you become an expert in direct-mail response so you can communicate these special needs to your designer.

In the final analysis, the design must be bold enough to attract the recipient's attention within the first three to five seconds. Secondly, it must "feel" right — that is, the recipient must feel that the overall visual image fits into his or her professional framework for taking in information. Third, the design must lead the reader through a story that culminates in asking for a response — a registration. Design and copy must all work together to achieve this end. There should be no higher goal for either design or copy.

Tip 56
Consider making use of a wide variety of additional services provided by most graphic designers.

Most graphic design firms, as well as free-lance graphic designers, provide helpful services other than just the actual graphic design. Some of these key services are to (1) arrange for typesetting, (2) deliver copy to the typesetters and collect the galleys to return to you for proofing, (3) arrange for free-lancers to proof galleys, (4) arrange for photographs, and (5) deliver camera-ready boards to the printers.

It is often more cost-effective in the long run to contract with graphic designers for some or all of these additional services. This saves you time, and it puts them in control of the entire design production process. If you wish to take advantage of these additional services, it is important that these be clearly spelled out in the letter of agreement with the designer. They are not usually considered to be part of the basic design service.

Tip 57
Take the time to build a long-term relationship with several graphic designers.

Nothing helps a working relationship with graphic designers like taking the time to build a lasting relationship. Take the time to educate them about your organization and its goals. Communicate clearly what overall image you want for your work—traditional, avant-garde, conservative, modern, forward thinking, or on the cutting edge of new ideas? Discuss how each of these approaches can best be communicated through graphic design.

Discuss your requirements for direct-mail response, and indicate your own preferences. For example, many program planners always insist on large, bold headlines for the program's title on the cover of a direct-mail brochure. If this is your preference, explain why this requirement must always be met.

Discuss research on direct-mail response. Indicate that your purpose is to elicit a favorable response from your recipients and that all design must lead toward this end. Discuss your own biases related to graphic design so that your designers can be aware of them.

Working with designers is very much a cooperative, two-way communication process. After you have worked with a designer on several projects, either you will begin to get on each other's wavelength or it will become clear that you are not in agreement on your design needs. Taking time to build a long-term relationship with several excellent graphic designers can save time and money, and eliminate hassles. A long-term relationship enables designers to give you the highest quality design possible to communicate your ideas in a way that enhances the overall image of your organization.

Tip 58
Generally use a minimum of different typefaces within the same direct-mail advertising piece.

There are hundreds of typefaces from which your graphic designer can choose to communicate your ideas effectively. In working with your designer, explain that you generally like to work with the same typeface for the bulk of your copy within a single project. While it may be appropriate to use different typefaces for emphasis and to attract attention, this variety tends to work best when kept to a minimum and used for a specific purpose— to attract attention. Sticking to a single typeface for the bulk of your copy increases readability, particularly for long sections of copy. It is usually best to use the same typeface for all these sections.

Tip 59
Consider carefully whether you want serif or sans-serif type.

Serif type has what are often called "little tails" at the ends of each letter. Sans-serif is a more modern typeface and does not have these little tails. Research studies show that serif type is easier to read than sans-serif, particularly for large amounts of copy.

Consider carefully whether your advertising should use serif or sans-serif type, and discuss this with your graphic designer. Ask to see samples of copy set in both serif and sans-serif typefaces that you and your designer are considering using. Be sure that your decision on using serif versus sans-serif is related to your overall design goals and is not done by default.

Tip 60
Consider carefully the size of type for the majority of your copy.

The point size of type refers to the height of the letters — 10-point type, for example, is smaller than 12-point type. For most people, 12-point type is easier to read than 10-point type. It is important to keep this in mind as you discuss your project with your graphic designer, particularly if your graphic designer is young and does not wear glasses. If this is the case, the designer may not personally be aware of how difficult smaller type is for some people to read.

A rule of thumb is that if a significant number of your target audience are over the age of forty, many of them will be wearing glasses with bifocals. If this is the case, it becomes even more important to use 10-point or larger type and to avoid using 9-point or anything smaller.

Tip 61
For direct-mail brochures, pay particular attention to the size of type in the general information section that tells how to register and describes program costs and other important details.

In many direct-mail brochures often you will see smaller type for this section. This is almost always a mistake. If you have an interested, motivated reader, the last thing you want to do is turn him or her off when you get to the general information section describing costs and how to register. This is some of your most important information. You may want to screen this section or draw a box around it for emphasis. However, it is almost always inappropriate to set the type in a smaller point size to save space. Doing this is one of the mistakes program planners most often make when developing their direct-mail advertising.

People who have to squint in order to read general information regarding costs, housing, and how to register will not be motivated to attend.

Tip 62
Choose an appropriate color of ink for the bulk of your advertising copy.

The easiest colors of ink to read are dark blue and black. It is really that simple. If you want to increase readability, any other color of ink for the body of your copy is almost always inappropriate. The exception might be dark brown or dark green. However, many direct-mail advertisers have come to feel that dark green ink tends to create somber, negative overtones to copy. And dark brown does not have the same readability as dark blue or black.

Other colors can be used effectively for emphasis in short headlines and to attract attention, but not for the bulk of your copy in a direct-mail brochure.

Tip 63
Do not use yellow ink for copy!

Yellow ink "bleeds" — that is, the edges of the yellow printing "bleed" into the color of the paper so that reading becomes difficult. There is a simple solution to this problem. Never use yellow ink for type under any circumstances!

Tip 64
Avoid using light pastel colors, even for emphasis.

Pastel colors also tend to bleed into the paper and decrease readability. In addition, they are usually too subtle to be used, even to attract attention to short words or phrases.

Tip 65
Generally avoid using metallic colors for copy.

The same guidelines apply to using metallic colors such as gold, silver, or bronze. When used for extensive sections of copy, the glare from the metallic color often makes printing very difficult to read, particularly on coated paper. If you do use gold, silver, or bronze metallic colors, use them only for emphasis — such as in logos or for headlines. Here these colors can be effective. They are generally not appropriate for advertising copy because readability is decreased and thus it becomes harder for the reader to receive the full impact of your message.

You never want to include any device that will decrease the ease with which your reader can take in your message.

Tip 66
Avoid reversing out large blocks of copy.

Reversing out is a process in which the background is printed with the color of ink being used — for example, black — while the copy is left with no color and thus becomes the color of the paper you are using. This technique can be very effective for creating emphasis for short words or phrases. However, it should never be used for copy longer than short headlines. When used for longer copy, reverse-outs become very hard to read because the contrast is too severe. Research on direct-mail advertising demonstrates that most people tend to skip over large blocks of reversed-out copy.

Tip 67
A good alternative to reverse-outs for longer pieces of copy is screening.

Screening means that the type is set in the color you have chosen for your copy — for example, dark blue. Then a box is drawn around the copy and the background is screened — that is, a light background is sprayed down, either in the color of the type for the copy or a different color. The most commonly used screens are 10 or 20 percent as background for copy. Any larger percentage tends to cause the printing to fade into the screen and thus decrease readability.

However, screening does tend to cut down on readability if it is used for the bulk of copy. Instead, use it for emphasis. For example, in a direct-mail brochure it is often used to emphasize the speakers' biographical statements, general information, or the phone number to call for more information.

Before using screening, always ask your graphic designer to show you an example of 10- and 20-percent screening so that you judge for yourself its readability and effectiveness for emphasis. Pay particular attention to any screening that is larger than 20 percent. If large amounts of copy are printed over any screening greater than 20 percent, it may be very difficult to read.

Hint: Avoid using a gray screen with black type. This often produces a dirty, washed-out look.

Tip 68
Using more than one color of ink for a direct-mail brochure has not proven to be a critical factor in increasing registrations.

Program planners who test colors of ink as a variable in increasing registrations often report that using more than one color is not the critical variable that increases registrations. However, there may be reasons other than the bottom line of being cost-effective that may affect the decision to use additional colors. For example, additional colors may be used to enhance the overall image of the program and its sponsoring organization. Multiple colors may lend a sense of increased importance and professionalism to the program.

You will want to consider the following issues before making decisions regarding how many colors to use on direct-mail advertising:

- What are the comparisons in cost for graphic design when preparing the camera-ready boards for one-, two-, three-, or four-color printing? For example, four-color printing demands additional graphic design preparation time.
- What are the differences in actual printing costs for more than one color?
- Is the extra expense affordable within the constraints of your program budget?
- Can the extra expense successfully be passed on to consumers through an increased registration fee that will cover additional costs for additional colors?

- How important is it to the program and your sponsoring organization to have more than one color to enhance your organizational and program image?

In making decisions about how many colors to use, it is important to test-market your particular type of direct-mail advertising using one, two, three, and four colors. In this way you will be able to develop your own data base to assist you in making decisions about how many colors to use to meet the overall marketing goals of your own organization.

Tip 69
Save money on printing by using only one color of ink but designing the project so that it creates the illusion that more than one color has been used.

If using more than one color for printing is beyond your budget, there are creative ways to use only one color but still create the illusion that you have used multiple colors. Consider the following possibilities:

- Use dark blue ink for printing on buff-colored paper. Have your graphic designer screen some of the copy with 10-percent screen for emphasis. For example, biographical copy about presenters at a workshop might have a 10-percent screen. Thus, you will have a light blue background against buff-colored paper for this section and still have dark blue printing over the light blue background. This creates the illusion you have used more than just one color when in reality you have not.
- Reverse out printing for bold headlines. Using this technique you could again use dark blue ink and buff-colored paper. Have the graphic designer integrate reverse-outs into the total design. You can create the illusion that several different colors have been used with this technique, combined with the type of screening mentioned above and the regular design of dark blue print on buff paper. A word of warning has already been given regarding reverse-outs. Do not reverse out large blocks of regular text because the contrast it creates makes copy very difficult to read. Instead use reverse-outs only for short, bold headlines.
- The above techniques can also be used very effectively with two colors. When this is done, you can usually create the visual illusion that three or four colors have been used.

If you have a limited budget, discuss these options with your graphic designer. Clearly state that you are on a limited budget but that you want the graphic designer to create the illusion that more than one color has been used. Designers can work wonders as they tackle this assignment and bring their best professional creativity to solving this problem.

Tip 70
When using photographs of program presenters, always be sure they are taken by professional photographers and show the presenters to their best professional advantage.

Picture the well-designed direct-mail brochure. The cover grabs your attention. The inside copy motivates you to want to attend. The presenters' biographical statements establish them as experts in their fields. And then come the presenters' photographs—fuzzy mug snapshots taken by amateurs. In addition, some of the men are wearing ties and others are wearing sport shirts. Some of the women presenters are wearing casual outfits, and others are wearing professional-looking suits or dresses.

Suddenly, the images in your mind of an excellent program begin to fade. Because of the photographs you quickly change your total image of the program. Now you view it as second-rate rather than excellent. It all happened in an instant because of the photographs.

To avoid this, follow these guidelines when using photographs in direct-mail advertising:

- Always have photographs taken by a professional photographer.
- If presenters are supplying their own photographs, explain to them why they must be taken by a professional.
- Show the person in the best possible professional way that is consistent with the content of the program—that is, the person should be dressed in a way that is considered professional for the target audience.
- Show the person in an action shot in his or her professional surroundings, if possible. This is generally more effective than a mug shot.
- Ask the photographer to provide you with high-contrast, glossy photographs. These reproduce best. Most photographers are used to providing glossy prints routinely; however, they have to receive special instructions to take high-contrast prints or they may not do so. Have a pointed discussion with your photographer to emphasize the need for high-contrast prints. This usually means that the person is photographed wearing dark clothes against a light background, or light-colored clothes against a dark background. In addition, the photographer must give special instructions to the photo processors to produce high-contrast, glossy prints. All photo processors know what this means and will work hard to fulfill this request. However, they can be most effective in doing this if the photographer has first been instructed to take photographs that will reproduce best for the high-contrast process.
- Having no photograph is better than using an amateur snapshot where the person is not dressed appropriately or using a photograph that does not have high contrast so that it will not reproduce well when printed.
- Be sure that all photographs are not more than three years old. Having presenters step in front of an audience when they are twenty-five years older than the photograph of them in a brochure is embarrassing.

Tip 71
When using group photographs in advertising to illustrate ideas, be aware to include an appropriate mix of males and females and people who represent the cultural diversity of your target audience.

Photographs are almost always more effective than hand-drawn artwork or clip art for advertising. This is because they are able to show real people in real situations interacting in ways designed to attract the attention of your potential program participants. Do not, however, fall into the trap of inadvertently alienating readers because they cannot find people like themselves in the pictures. For example, a review of 150 direct-mail brochures advertising conferences and workshops recently revealed the following mistakes in the use of photographs:

• For a program entitled "How to Build Executive Teams in Your Organization," photographs of teams of executives were used liberally throughout the brochure. The high-contrast photographs were clearly taken by a professional. The people were seen in action shots that showed them in their actual work situations engaging in team activities. There was only one problem — all the executives pictured were white men. Women were shown only as secretaries in relation to male executives. No minority members were represented visually in the executive ranks. Therefore, the total advertising piece inadvertently alienated female executives as well as nonwhite executives, who did not register for the program because of the negative visual message.

• For a program entitled "Working with Distressed Families" designed for social workers, photographs of families in action-shot situations were used. However, all of the families pictured were white. Thus, the visual message of the advertising did not communicate the cultural diversity with which all members of the target audience dealt on a daily basis.

Two messages are clear. First, it is essential to include members of both sexes in photographs when the target group of program registrants includes members of both sexes. Second, it is important to consider cultural diversity in photographs so that as many people as possible in your target audience can see people with whom they can identify on an intuitive, personal basis.

Tip 72
Select paper stock so that it will enhance the image of your program.

There are thousands of different types of paper stocks that can be used for printing. These include everything from newsprint to heavily coated stock that has a rich, expensive look and feel. Consider carefully the target audience for your advertising. Are they presidents of large businesses? If so, they will probably view a direct-mail brochure on "Time Management for the Busy Executive" printed on newsprint as not being for them. However, they will be more likely to pay attention to the identical brochure printed on heavy stock that has a rich look and feel to it.

Here is a useful guideline to consider when choosing paper: Assume that members of your target audience get four brochures for the same type of program on the same day. What is it about your brochure, including the quality of paper, that will make the person read your message, register, and thus reject the competition? If you keep this in mind, decisions about paper stock become easier.

Work with your graphic designers on the selection of paper stock. They will have many samples that you can look at and touch.

Tip 73
Color of paper is an important consideration.

Here the guidelines are clear. Consider what has to be printed on the paper. If you have a direct-mail brochure that has a lot of copy and you want your reader to be able to read it easily, you have two foolproof choices for paper color—white or buff-colored paper. Using any other color runs the risk of decreasing readability. The following represents a short summary of errors made in selection of paper color as a result of reviewing over 500 direct-mail advertising brochures for meetings:

• A brochure printed on dark gray stock with black printing. The image was too somber. It looked like an announcement for a funeral. In addition, it was extremely difficult to read the copy without squinting or taking the brochure to a brightly lit area.

• A brochure printed on dark, rust-colored stock with silver printing. In addition to the color of paper stock making the printing difficult to read, the shine from the metallic silver printing made the copy doubly hard to read. Incidentally, a number of brochures during that particular year were printed on this color of stock with metallic silver ink. It appeared to be the "in" color that year. Warning: Stay away from any year's "in" colors.

• A brochure printed on pink paper with medium gray printing. This is another designer-color mistake in which the year's "in" colors were used. Medium gray printing does not have enough contrast for large amounts of copy to be read quickly and with ease. Printing for this type of brochure should have been in either black or dark blue.

• A brochure with dark green printing on light green paper. Here the contrast between the color of the printing and the paper stock was not enough to ensure good readability. Thus, the visual image of the brochure was washed-out and blah.

Again, the safest way to go to ensure readability is to use white or buff-colored paper with black or dark blue printing for large blocks of copy. While other colors of ink are often appropriate to add emphasis and thus serve to gain attention, they should not be used for large blocks of copy.

Tip 74
To save money, arrange with your typesetter to receive all copy from your computer's word processing program directly from a disk or via modem over phone lines.

This will have the following three important payoffs for you:

1. It will cut your typesetting bills approximately in half because no one has to rekey copy into the typesetting machine.
2. If you run a computer spelling check first, it should be possible to eliminate typographical errors due to spelling.
3. You will get faster turnaround on typesetting—usually within twenty-four hours.

The easiest way to accomplish this is to have your graphic designer mark up printed copy, also called *hard copy,* to indicate style, point size of type, and spacing requirements. Then take the data along with the marked-up hard copy to the typesetter on a disk or send it via telephone modem. The typesetter will insert the proper codes for style of type, point size, and spacing into the text as indicated on the marked-up hard copy. You can work with the typesetter to learn these codes and insert them yourself, but most program planners and graphic designers find it is more cost-effective to have the professionals at the typesetters do this.

Hint: Although it virtually eliminates spelling errors if you run a spell-check on your computer, read the typeset galleys very carefully anyway. Mistakes can always creep into this process. Also, computer spelling checkers cannot distinguish incorrect spelling because of usage—such as the correct form of *to, too,* or *two,* depending on the way the word is used in a sentence.

Tip 75
In order to save time and money, be sure that all corrections on copy have been made before any of it goes to the graphic designer and then on to the typesetter.

One of the mistakes most often made in the direct-mail production process is deciding after copy has been typeset to make substantive changes other than to correct errors made in the typesetting process. For example, it is not uncommon for program planners to have brochure copy typeset and then make major changes in wording on most of the copy. This costs both time and money.

In order to avoid this, establish the principle in your office that all copy must be proofed and completely agreed upon before it is typeset. This means that several people should critique and proof copy and that all rewrites should be completed. When you are satisfied that you have produced the best possible copy and that you will not make any other changes, send it to the graphic designer.

Changes you make after copy has been typeset are costly and time-consuming. Any major, substantive changes can easily double your typesetting bill as well as delay your production process, so avoiding them saves you money.

Tip 76
Never, under any circumstances, produce a direct-mail brochure in any size smaller than 8½ by 11 inches.

The world is used to doing business in the 8½-by-11-inch format. Any brochure that is smaller will look insignificant in relation to the other mail potential registrants receive. It is that simple. Avoid at all costs what is often referred to as the "small, three-fold brochure." This is a brochure that is 8½-by-11 inches unfolded but has been folded down twice to form three panels. Direct-mail brochures of this size look cheap, they are ineffective, they do not speak to the quality your organization wants to be known for, and they should never be used unless you are in the process of declaring bankruptcy and wish to hasten the process to get the agony over with.

The minimum size for effective direct-mail brochures for advertising conferences and workshops should be four 8½-by-11-inch pages unfolded. Larger brochures can be equally effective.

Tip 77
Always get several estimates for all printing jobs before selecting a printer.

Printers vary in their prices for jobs, so always get several estimates before deciding. Remember, the lowest bid is not necessarily your best deal. The following are the major factors governing prices printers will quote:

- Often a printer who has some slack time will offer a better price for a particular printing date than one who has many printing jobs scheduled for that date. The thinking here is that they would like to make less money during slack times than no money at all.
- Printers typically have a variety of paper stocks on hand. Thus, if you can use paper from their regular stock, you usually can get a lower printing bid than if the printer has to special order your paper.
- If a printer has leftover paper, you can sometimes get a real bargain. Paper left over from other print jobs does a printer no good. Often they will be willing to quote a lower price for your project if you can use their overstock. Consider inquiring about this as part of your discussions related to all print jobs.
- Not all printers have the same experience with all types of printing. For example, some printers may not specialize in four-color printing. If this is the case, the last thing you want to do is experiment with a printer who has not had a great deal of four-color experience just because you can get a lower price.

Printers are used to the competitive bid process, so they will be glad to quote you prices for each of your projects. Then you can decide which one to use. But remember that price is not the only consideration.

Tip 78
Always ask to see a blueline before giving the printer permission to print your job.

You have checked your camera-ready boards prepared by your graphic designer. They are perfect, so you give your okay to print and the designer delivers the boards to the printers. However, you cannot assume that nothing will go wrong between this step and the final printing. Many errors can still creep into the process. For example, an additional word or letter that has been pasted on the boards can fall off. Dust can get on the boards or the photographic plates, which will reproduce as tiny flecks of ink on your printing.

To ensure that these errors do not creep into the process, always ask to see a blueline before giving the printer permission to go to final printing. A blueline, sometimes called a *silverline* or a *mechanical,* is a photograph of exactly what your printing will look like in its final form. This is your last chance to catch any errors that may have taken place after your camera-ready boards were delivered to the printers. Proof the blueline carefully. The most common mistakes you will find are as follows:

- Dust particles that appear as tiny flecks on the paper. Mark these carefully so that the printer can take these out. What you see on the blueline is what you get on your final printing.
- Incomplete or fuzzy printing on an individual letter or whole word. Often this appears as a tail that is left off of an individual letter of serif type. Mark these errors.
- Photographs that appear fuzzy. If they are fuzzy on the blueline, they will be fuzzy on the final printed copy. Mark these. Naturally photographs that are fuzzy on the original cannot be corrected at this point.
- Fuzziness on artwork. Mark this.
- Breaks in solid lines. Note these.
- Bold printing that appears fuzzy. This is an error that can be corrected by the printer.

If you find any errors on the blueline, insist that meticulous corrections be made. What you see is what you get in this case. The blueline represents exactly what you will get in the final printed copy except for color. All the printing on a blueline is usually light blue against a buff-colored special paper.

Note: The blueline is not the time to do your first thorough proofreading. This should be done at the galley stage before any copy is pasted up on the boards. Correcting errors on a blueline, such as proofreading errors that are your fault, is very expensive as well as time-consuming. The purpose of the blueline check is to check for errors the printer has made.

Tip 79
If errors have to be corrected on the blueline, insist on a second blueline to check.

Do not assume that errors will get corrected just because you marked them. Ask to see a second blueline along with the original showing the errors you marked. Check carefully to ensure that all marked errors have actually been corrected. Do not give your permission to print until you are satisfied that the blueline represents the printer's highest quality and is completely error-free.

Tip 80
Any errors you do not catch on the blueline are considered to be your responsibility.

Most printers will ask you to initial each page of the final blueline to indicate that you have reviewed their work and find it to be acceptable at that stage. Even if they do not ask you to actually initial a blueline, giving your verbal approval to print is the same thing. If you have not marked an error on the blueline and you later find an error on the final printed product that can be shown to have appeared on the blueline, legally the printer is absolved from all responsibility for adjustments.

Tip 81
If you receive inferior work from a printer, ask the printer to reprint your entire job.

Do not ever accept inferior work from a printer. Most printers are very conscientious and want only to produce the very highest quality of work. However, because printing is a very complex process, mistakes do happen. Consider the following example: A printer produced 60,000 four-color, eight-page brochures for a conference. The color separations on the front cover were off by a fraction of an inch. As a result, the printing and photographs appeared slightly fuzzy. To compensate for this, the printer offered to reduce the bill by $3,000.

Do not accept such an offer. You will be sending out an inferior piece of advertising that will create a negative impression with your reader. Insist that the printer reprint to correct the mistake at no cost to you.

Tip 82
Arrange with printers ahead of time on the quality control methods they will use.

It is easy for errors to occur in jobs, even when the printer has taken all measures possible to control quality. Therefore, to ensure that all of your printing is of the same high quality, work out with your printer in advance exactly what quality control checking measures will be used. For example, one way to do this is to have the printer assure you that they will pull one printed piece in approximately every hundred to check for quality control.

Tip 83
Also institute a quality control check yourself when you receive your printed materials.

Even though your printer has guaranteed that quality control measures have been used, it is important for you to conduct a similar check whenever possible. Therefore, if the printed pieces are delivered to you, conduct a random check to see if all the printing quality is excellent.

If the printer delivers your printing directly to a mailing house, and this is often the case for very large mailings because you probably do not have adequate space to receive and store large projects, you can go to the print shop and conduct a quality control check yourself before the job is shipped out to a mailing house.

Hint: Doing this will also ensure that the printer has actually printed the amount you ordered. For very large jobs, it is easy for printers to under-print. Often this will not be discovered until the shipment is being labeled at a mailing house, if it is discovered at all. When this happens, completing your mailing can be delayed by a number of days while additional printing is done. Then the mailing house has to gear up for processing this additional printing. This can delay a project for up to two weeks, and most direct-mail advertising projects do not have this amount of time to spare if they are to be as effective as possible.

Summary

Achieving excellence with graphic design, typesetting, and printing is important to the overall success of your organization. The tips in this chapter have been summarized and condensed from what is considered excellent professional practice in planning conferences and workshops. The checklist in Exhibit 16 serves as a summary of items to consider to ensure quality in this area.

Exhibit 16. Checklist for Establishing Quality and Excellence in Graphic Design, Typesetting, and Printing.

As you review this list, modify it to include all the essential elements you need to consider for producing excellence in graphic design, typesetting, and printing.

Working with a Graphic Designer

_____ 1. Employ a professional graphic designer for your advertising projects.

_____ 2. Secure a letter of agreement from the graphic designer stating the terms and services to be provided for each project.

_____ 3. Consider using your graphic designer for a wide variety of services such as taking projects to the typesetters and printers and proofing copy.

_____ 4. Build a long-term relationship with several graphic designers.

Issues Related to Typeface and Size

_____ 5. Use a minimum of different type faces within any one advertising piece.

_____ 6. Decide whether serif or sans-serif type is most appropriate.

_____ 7. Use 10- or 12-point type for the bulk of copy text, preferably 12-point.

_____ 8. Be sure that the general information section that contains information about times, place, price, and how to register is in type that can be easily read, even by people with bifocals. (This usually means 10- or 12-point type, with 9-point type being the minimum size that should be used.)

Choosing Colors of Ink

_____ 9. The bulk of all text copy in a direct-mail brochure should be black or dark blue for the easiest readability.

_____ 10. Do not use yellow ink for copy! It "bleeds" and cannot be read easily.

_____ 11. Avoid other light pastel inks for copy.

_____ 12. Avoid metallic colored ink for large blocks of text.

_____ 13. Avoid reversing out large blocks of text.

_____ 14. A good alternative to reverse-outs for large blocks of text is screening at 10 or 20 percent.

_____ 15. Using more than one color of ink is usually not the critical variable that will increase registrations.

_____ 16. To save money, work with your graphic designer to find creative ways to create the illusion that more than one color of ink has been used.

**Exhibit 16. Checklist for Establishing Quality and
Excellence in Graphic Design, Typesetting, and Printing, Cont'd.**

Using Photographs and Artwork

_____ 17.   Employ a professional photographer for producing quality pictures in all advertising.

_____ 18.   Always create a mixture of males and females in pictures if your target audience contains males and females.

_____ 19.   Always consider the cultural diversity of your target audience and reflect this in all photographs.

_____ 20.   Be sure to use current photographs.

_____ 21.   Always order high-contrast, glossy prints from the photograph processor.

Choosing Paper Stock

_____ 22.   Select paper stock that compliments the image and quality of your program.

_____ 23.   White or buff-colored paper provides the best background for easy-to-read printing.

Working with a Typesetter and Printer

_____ 24.   Save money by arranging with your typesetter to receive copy on a computer disk. This avoids having to rekey text.

_____ 25.   Be sure that everyone agrees to all corrections on copy before any of it goes to the graphic designer.

_____ 26.   Never produce any direct-mail brochure that is smaller than 8½ by 11 inches.

_____ 27.   Always get competitive bids for each project before selecting a printer.

_____ 28.   Carefully review as many bluelines as necessary to guarantee a flawless final printed product.

_____ 29.   If you receive inferior work from any printer, ask to have your job reprinted at the printer's expense.

_____ 30.   Institute your own checking procedures to ensure quality control on all jobs. For example, check every hundredth item.

Source: Planning and Marketing Conferences and Workshops: Tips, Tools, and Techniques, by Robert G. Simerly. San Francisco: Jossey-Bass. Copyright ©1990. Permission granted to reproduce.

4

Predicting Costs and Revenues:

Twenty-Eight Tips for Developing Accurate and Realistic Budgets

Nothing is more important to the overall success of programs than planning and managing successful budgets. This chapter explores ways to plan and manage program budgets so that financial management of programs can be as successful as program planning and marketing. Guidelines for budget development are presented, and a simple, easy-to-use budget form that is equally effective for small or large programs is included. It contains all the essential items found in most program budgets and can easily be modified to suit your individual needs. In addition, it can quickly be adapted to an electronic spreadsheet on a personal computer. A series of tips on how to avoid the most often made mistakes in the budgeting process is also provided.

This chapter is written for the person who is required to manage program budgets but who has never had an accounting course. In order to follow the concepts presented, this chapter should be read sequentially. Begin at the beginning and do not skip around among the tips, because the illustrations and the sample budgets that are presented are referred to in tips throughout the chapter.

These practical budgeting tips have been tested in large and small organizations. They work equally well whether you are planning a program for 20 people that will last one day or a program for 5,000 people that will last a week and has a registration fee of $1,500. In addition, they work equally well whether you plan conferences and workshops for higher education, professional associations, or corporations. The financial management principles remain the same. Implement these principles and guidelines and you will be assured of successful budgeting for your programs.

Tip 84
Make clear distinctions among budget planning, accounting, and financial management.

The business of successful financial management has a specialized language. Therefore, it is important to make distinctions among three important terms — *budget planning, accounting,* and *financial management. Budget planning* refers to the upfront work of planning a budget from the beginning. It includes such elements as identifying all expenses, estimating all income, and deciding on a break-even point. *Accounting* is the term used to describe the accounting, or keeping track, of all income as it enters your bookkeeping system and all expenses as they are paid from your account. *Financial management* is the large, umbrella term that refers to the overall way in which you plan budgets, account for income and expenses, and report your findings in a way that can be easily understood.

It is important to keep these distinctions in mind throughout the budget planning and management cycle of any program. In this way, you can clearly distinguish among the three as you work with planning groups, staff, clients, and any other important groups that may be key stakeholders in the overall success of a program.

Tip 85
Planning and managing successful budgets involves more than just the mathematical calculation of the individual items in a budget.

Administering successful budgets requires good negotiating skills, a clear sense of the goals for each budget, a check and balance system that monitors all expenses, and a good record-keeping system. All of these variables work together to constitute a successful approach to budgeting. Bringing a positive attitude to the budget planning process is also important. This is especially true when working with clients or planning groups. Negotiating a successful budget in a positive manner requires time and a thorough identification of all anticipated expenses and revenues.

Tip 86
Develop clear goals for financial management.

It is important to develop clear goals for the budgeting process of a single program as well as for the overall management of your organization's financial resources. Goals are large, generalized statements that help provide a direction or vision for the organization. Establishing overall goals for each program budget as well as for the total budget for your office is an important first step in successful financial planning. For example, the following financial goals are appropriate for almost all organizations planning conferences and workshops.

- To develop a uniform system for planning all program budgets — a system that can easily be understood and learned by all staff
- To plan and manage budgets so there will be no surprises at the end of the year
- To develop a system for monitoring budget records — a system that can be easily be updated every twenty-four hours so that an accurate accounting of all income and expenses can be maintained.

After clear financial goals have been established for the overall office budget, it is possible to establish clear goals for individual program budgets. Usually each separate program budget will have only one financial goal — to break even according to the items listed on the budgeting form.

Tip 87
Conceptualize the budget planning process.

There are five major steps involved in creating an individual program budget. These steps divide the budget planning into logical increments that can be discussed and analyzed.

1. Identify accurately all expenses associated with a program.
2. Clearly distinguish between fixed and variable expenses.
3. Determine how many people can be expected to attend so that a break-even point can be established.
4. Establish a registration fee that is equal to or exceeds the total fixed and variable expenses incurred for each registrant.
5. Display budget data so that the logic of how the registration fee was established can be easily understood.

Thinking of each program budget as having these five distinct steps makes it possible to analyze and develop specific strategies for managing each step.

Tip 88
Develop a clear set of guidelines for what breaking even financially means.

Budgets for all programs should be designed to break even. The problem is that the term *break even* can have a number of different meanings, depending on the set of assumptions governing the accounting procedures for any given program. For example, here are two issues to consider in order to develop a satisfactory definition of the term *break even:*

- Breaking even can be simply a matter of ensuring that all direct expenses for a program end up being equal to or less than income generated through registration fees.
- Breaking even can also mean recovering indirect costs for such expenses as staff time, utilities in your building, and other office expenses. When recovering these indirect costs, the term *break even* has a very different meaning and any final budget wrap-up will look quite different. For example, listed below are the typical kinds of indirect costs that often need to be recovered, along with estimates for the purpose of illustration.

Staff time devoted to running the program	$4,000
Fringe benefits @ 23% of salary	1,320
Utilities	250
Phones	175
General office supplies	550
Total	$6,295

Thus, in this example in order to break even you need to include $6,295 in additional expenses. For budgeting purposes, this is called an *administrative fee*.

Tip 89
Always distinguish clearly between fixed and variable expenses in any budget.

It is not possible to ascertain the break-even point in a budget and display this information in a clear, easy-to-understand format unless fixed and variable costs are always kept separate. This is the important first step in building a successful budget. *Fixed expenses* are those expenses that will remain the same no matter how many people come to your program. For example, printing costs for a direct-mail brochure will remain the same no matter how many people attend because you made this commitment up front as part of your overall direct-mail strategy. *Variable expenses* will vary according to the number of people who attend. For example, meals are a variable expense. If 100 people attend a program, you will need to order and pay for 100 lunches. On the other hand, if only 25 people attend, you will only need to order and pay for 25 lunches.

The following are some of the most commonly found examples of fixed and variable expense items:

Fixed Expenses

Printing of direct-mail advertising
Honoraria paid to program presenters
Travel expenses for presenters
Mailing of brochures
Graphic design and typesetting for direct-mail brochures

Rental of mailing lists
Advertising in newspapers or magazines
Equipment rental
Photography

Variable Expenses

Registration packets
Meals
Coffee breaks
Duplication of items included in registration packets
Paper and pencils given out to participants

It is important to keep in mind that it is impossible to plan a successful budget if fixed and variable expenses are not always kept separate as part of the budget planning process.

Tip 90
Display budget data in a clear, concise format that separates fixed and variable expenses.

For planning purposes, it is important to develop a way to display budget data so that they are clear and can be understood by everyone involved with the program planning process. The budget form in Exhibit 17 shows a good way to do this.

Exhibit 17. Program Budget Form.

Account					
Number:	58475	Program Number:	3746		
Submitted by:	*Wilma Carr*	Date:	3/3/89		

Course Title: *Executive Leadership Development Program*

Course Dates: 2/3/89 To 2/7/89

Instruction Payroll and Travel
(Fringe Benefits to Be Paid)

Instructor	Travel	Per Diem	Honorarium	Other	Total
Margaret West			1,500		1,500
Wessley Masters			1,500		1,500
Linda Miels			1,500		1,500
James Brabson			1,500		1,500
					0
Total Instructors	0	0	6,000	0	6,000
Benefits at 20%			1,200		1,200
Total	0	0	7,200	0	7,200

(Fringe Benefits Not to Be Paid)

Instructor	Travel	Per Diem	Honorarium	Other	Total
Max Stern	500	150	1,500	75	2,225
Tamera Sands	600	200	1,500	75	2,375
					0
					0
					0
Total Other Instructors	1,100	350	3,000	150	4,600
Total Instructors	1,100	350	10,200	150	11,800

Exhibit 17. Program Budget Form, Cont'd.

Fixed Expenses	Amount	Per Person Variable Expenses	Amount
Planning Committee	100	Registration Pack	2.00
Typesetting	200	Notebook	10.00
List Purchase	650	Paper/Pencils	1.00
Advertising	1,200	Per Person Duplicating	15.00
Printing	5,000	Per Person Administrative Fee	50.00
Graphic Design	300	Other:	
		Registration Fee	5.24
		8 coffee breaks @1.25	10.00
		4 lunches @15	60.00
Mailing/Postage	4,675	4 dinners @19	76.00
		Total Variable Expenses	229.24
Entertainment	200		
Photography	100		
Equipment Rental	200		
Equipment Moving	75		
Physical Plant	45		
Complimentary Expenses	917		
Other			
Instruction (page 1)	11,800		
Administrative Fee	3,000		
Total Fixed Expenses	28,462		

Fixed Expense Summary

Total Fixed Expenses		28,462
Misc. @ %	10%	2,846
Total Fixed		31,308
Projected Attendance		25
Fixed Expenses/Person		1,252

Registration Fee Calculation	
Per Person Fixed	1,252
Per Person Variable	229.24
Total per Person	1,482
Add: Credit Card @ 4%	59
Total per Person Expenses	1,541
Registration Fee	1,550

Approved by: _____

Date: _____

Note that the budget planning form is clear and concise. All expenses for instruction, which include travel, per diem, and honoraria, are grouped together. These are fixed expenses. Note that if you need to pay fringe benefits to presenters, these salaries are listed separately from presenters to whom you do not have to pay fringe benefits. The total amount in this category for the Executive Leadership Program is $11,800, which is displayed at the bottom of the "Instruction Payroll and Travel" section in Exhibit 17. There follows a listing of the fixed expenses, to include such categories as planning committee meetings, typesetting, printing, mailing, and equipment rental. This category also contains a fixed expense category of $3,000 for an administrative fee. More will be said about this administrative fee cost recovery later in the chapter. Thus, as can be seen in the "Fixed Expenses" section of the exhibit, the subtotal of fixed expenses for this program is estimated to be $28,462. To this is added 10 percent as a miscellaneous category to take care of all additional unforeseen expenses. This brings the total of the fixed expenses to $31,308.

Next, in the right-hand column of the exhibit, per person variable expenses are listed. These will vary depending on the number of people who attend. The total variable expenses identified are $229.24 per person.

The registration fee calculation box at the bottom of the left column of the exhibit shows how to use the break-even number of twenty-five people to convert the fixed fee expenses to a per person cost recovery. This is calculated as $31,308 divided by twenty-five people, which results in $1,252 of each registration fee that must go toward paying fixed expenses. To this add $229.24 to account for the variable per person expenses. If you plan to allow registrants to charge their fee to a credit card, figure in the percentage you must pay the bank for this service. In Exhibit 17 it is 4 percent. This adds another $59 to each registration fee, for a total per person expense of $1,541. Thus, the registration fee is set at $1,550, with twenty-five people needed to break even.

Tip 91
Include fringe benefits as expenses if appropriate.

Depending on the type of organization for which you work, you may or may not have to pay fringe benefits to presenters. These fringe benefits cover retirement, social security, and health insurance. In many organizations, fringe benefits can be up to 35 percent of compensation. Therefore, when planning all budgets, carefully calculate any fringe benefits that must be paid.

Tip 92
Remember to include tax and gratuity for all meals.

In the figures for meals in Exhibit 17, tax and gratuity have been included in the meal figures. Since this can often amount to up to 30 percent additional, be sure to include the appropriate amounts as part of your expenses listed for each meal and for coffee breaks. This may either be figured in as part of the total meal cost, as has been done in Exhibit 17, or be listed as a separate item under the per person variable expenses.

Tip 93
Calculate complimentary registrations as fixed expenses.

One mistake frequently made in planning budgets is to forget that there is no such thing as a free registration. Complimentary registrations do not cost the people receiving them anything, but as Exhibit 17 shows, the per person variable expenses for the Executive Leadership Development Program are $229.24. This means that every complimentary registration actually costs the sponsoring organization $229.24.

In planning for this as part of the total budget, complimentary registrations must be converted to fixed expenses. For example, in Exhibit 17, four complimentary registrations were given. Thus, the total fixed expenses in this category were calculated as 4 × $229.24, which rounds off to a total of $917. This is listed as a fixed expense in Exhibit 17 under the category "Complimentary Expenses."

As the budget planning sheet in Exhibit 17 demonstrates, it is imperative to decide before any registration fee is established exactly how many complimentary registrations you wish to give. These then become fixed expenses that must be recovered as part of other fixed expenses.

Tip 94
Carefully calculate the costs for everything that will be given out at the program.

Items that are often given to program participants are a registration packet, pencils, pens, paper, program booklets, pamphlets, and other duplicated materials. Because each of these items has a real cost to you as the sponsor, it is essential to decide exactly what will be given out as part of the registration materials so that these expenses can be figured in as part of the per person variable expenses. Do not wait until a week before the program to decide this very important issue. It must be considered as part of the total budget planning process.

Tip 95
Always plan a percentage for miscellaneous expenses.

All programs have expenses that will be incurred between the time the budget has been agreed to and the time the program actually takes place.

Therefore, always plan to add at least 10 percent to all fixed expenses to account for these last-minute, unplanned expenses. Depending on the type of program you run or the type of organization for which you work, it may be necessary to add a higher figure for miscellaneous expenses. This miscellaneous category becomes your safeguard against rising prices and unforeseen additional expenses, as well as for additional items you would like to include as part of the program that you did not think of until the budget had been established.

Tip 96
Include charges for credit card registrations as a separate expense item.

Many providers of conferences and workshops find that over half of their attendees register by credit card. If you make use of credit card registrations, be sure to figure in the percentage of each registration fee you must pay the bank for this service. For example, in Exhibit 17, the percentage was calculated at 4 percent of each registration fee.

Hint: For budget planning purposes it is important always to assume that all registrants will take advantage of the credit card charge option. Do not try to figure out what percentage will and will not register by credit card because you have no reliable way of estimating this variable over which you have no control. In order to build a fail-safe budget, you must assume for your planning purposes that all participants will register by credit card.

Tip 97
Use historical records to build a reliable data base for calculating a successful break-even point for each program.

Calculating a reliable break-even point for any program can be difficult. In fact, one of the mistakes most often made in budget planning is overestimating the number of people who can be counted on to register for a program. Therefore, it is important to develop a research base related to your own programs in order to successfully estimate break-even attendance.

For example, if historical records show that most executive development workshops you have sponsored register an average of fifty people, you can assume with a fair degree of reliability that your future programs will attract fifty people too. However, never use your average attendance figures to calculate a break-even figure. Instead, use average attendance figures and then cut this to 30 to 50 percent in order to plan for a worst-case scenario. Thus, if your programs usually attract fifty people, assume a worst-case scenario for the one coming up. Use your historical registration number and cut it by 40 percent to figure a break-even point. This would mean that you would figure a budget using thirty as the number of registrations required to break even, although your historical records show that you will probably attract fifty people.

Tip 98
If you are working with other people, such as a planning committee or a client, to sponsor the program, always have them sign the budget form to indicate their agreement and acceptance of the budget figures.

If you are running the program yourself, it means that you assume all the risks and benefit from all the gains. Thus, this signature will not be necessary. However, you may be working with planning committees, clients, and other sponsoring groups who need input into the budgeting process. When this is the case, always have the appropriate people sign the budget form to indicate that everyone agrees to the terms and the budget estimates. This can go a long way to avoid misunderstandings later. For example, one of the typical misunderstandings concerns complimentary registrations.

Take the case of a university academic department planning a large conference for 2,000 people. The group agreed during discussions that no complimentary registrations would be given, and the appropriate representatives signed the budget form. However, after the direct-mail brochures went out and registrations began to be received, the members of the faculty in the academic department began to insist on complimentary registrations for themselves. A major crisis developed over this issue, with faculty requesting fifty-four complimentary registrations that would have covered all members of the department. The per person variable costs for the program were $214 each. Therefore, fifty-four complimentary registrations at $214 would result in $11,556 in additional, unplanned expenses. Having a signed budget form containing the signatures of the appropriate designated decision makers to indicate what the upfront agreements had been quickly resolved the disagreement.

Tip 99
Create a spreadsheet to display important data needed to plan an entire year's schedule of programs.

If you just do one conference a year, this tip is not for you. However, if you work in an office that plans a number of conferences and workshops each year, in order to do the best possible job of planning your entire year's finances, it is important to create an electronic spreadsheet on a personal computer so you can create alternative scenarios for the income and expenses related to your entire office. Exhibit 18 shows how to do this.

Without a spreadsheet similar to the one in Exhibit 18, it is impossible to decide on the appropriate administrative fee to charge for each program. In addition, it is impossible to develop a year's budget for the entire office.

Exhibit 18. Spreadsheet for Yearly Planning.

Yearly Budget

	A	B	C	D
1				
2	How to Plan Income and Expenses for an Entire Year			
3				
4	Projected Office Expenses			
5		Salaries		
6			Wilcox, Wilma	$40,269.00
7			Sampson, Linda	$45,821.00
8			Maxxon, William	$35,298.00
9			Streternot, James	$38,678.00
10				
11			Subtotal	$160,066.00
12			Fringe Benefits @ 25%	$40,016.50
13				
14			Total Salaries	$200,082.50
15				
16		General Office Expenses		
17			Telephones	$9,250.00
18			Copying Machine Lease	$6,230.00
19			General Supplies	$12,000.00
20			Equipment Purchase	$7,800.00
21			Equipment Maintenance	$8,000.00
22			Heating	$11,000.00
23			Electricity	$9,250.00
24			Water	$1,000.00
25			Office Rental	$15,000.00
26			General Travel	$8,500.00
27			Entertaining	$5,000.00
28			Staff Development	$6,000.00
29				
30			Subtotal	$99,030.00
31				
32			Total Salaries and	$299,112.50
33			Office Expenses	
34				
35			Add 10% Miscellaneous	$29,911.25
36				
37			Total Expenses	$329,023.75

Exhibit 18. Spreadsheet for Yearly Planning, Cont'd.

Yearly Programs

	A	B	C	D	E	F	G
1							
2							
3	Projected Programs for the Year	1	2	3	4	5	6
4			Projected	Projected	Administrative	Total Net	Total Contributed Toward All Office Expenses
5	Name of program	Dates	Income	Expenses	Cost Recovery	Balance	(Add Columns 4 and 5)
6							
7	Income Tax Institute	May 3-5	$38,750	$38,750	$3,000	$0	$3,000
8	International Conference on Pesticides	June 7-10	$789,223	$650,261	$15,000	$138,962	$153,962
9	Family Living Conference	June 15-20	$562,015	$402,915	$25,218	$159,100	$184,318
10	National Marketing Conference	July 14-17	$210,000	$185,623	$8,000	$24,377	$32,377
11	Workshop for High School Leadership	August 15-28	$30,000	$25,352	$3,500	$4,648	$8,148
12	Update on Tax Laws for CPAs	October 8-19	$158,000	$142,000	$10,000	$16,000	$26,000
13	Economic Development for Government	November 15	$256,000	$245,000	$6,000	$11,000	$17,000
14							
15		Totals	$2,043,988	$1,689,901	$70,718	$354,087	$424,805
16							
17							
18	Summary Information	Total Projected	$329,024				
19		Office Expenses					
20							
21		Total Cost	$424,805				
22		Recovery					
23							
24		Balance	$95,781				Thus, the statement that can be made is that the office is projected to generate
25				$95,781 more than it anticipates in total expenses			
26							

The first part of the spreadsheet in Exhibit 18 displays an estimate of all office expenses for a fiscal year. Note that fringe benefits are included for salaries. Also note that there is a line item amount listed for all general expenses, from telephones to staff development. To the total of salaries and office expenses of $299,112.50 is added 10 percent for miscellaneous. *Hint:* Any budget should always have a miscellaneous category to account for unforeseen expenses. In Exhibit 18 this has been calculated as 10 percent because historical evidence suggests this to be an accurate estimate. This brings the total estimated expenses for the year to $329,024.

Next on the spreadsheet comes the laying out of a total year's programs. In column C income is projected and in column D expenses are projected. In column E the administrative fee cost recovery is listed. Column G is calculated as the sum of column E plus any additional positive or negative balance in column F. For example, in the second listing, the International Conference on Pesticides, the following statement can be made. Out of the $650,261 in projected expenses, $15,000 of these expenses were for the administrative fee cost recovery. In addition, $138,962 was made, for a total net balance of $153,962 that can be applied toward covering the office expenses for the year.

Later in the spreadsheet we note that the total cost recovery for all programs is projected to be $424,805. This is balanced against $329,024 in projected expenses. Thus, the office is projected to be able to pay all of its expenses for the year plus create an additional $95,781 profit.

An important assumption behind this spreadsheet is that a detailed budget similar to the one in Exhibit 18 has been developed for each program. This is the only reliable way to develop the estimates for projected income and expenses on the spreadsheet in Exhibit 18. Without detailed, carefully planned individual budgets there is no reliable way to estimate what an entire year of business will net.

Tip 100
Plan for recovering your staff and office expenses through an administrative fee.

Many organizations must recover some or all of their overhead expenses to pay for salaries and other office expenses. Typically this overhead recovery is achieved through an administrative fee charged to each program. The methods most often used for recovering these fees are the following:

- *Flat administrative fee.* This is a flat fee that is figured as part of the fixed expenses on the budget sheet. For example, in Exhibit 17 the flat administrative fee is $3,000. Exhibit 18 shows how these administrative fees plus additional money are combined for a total cost recovery that can be used to pay for office expenses.
- *Per person variable fee.* In this method a per person variable fee for administrative cost recovery is charged in the per person variable fee column

of the budget form. Exhibit 17 shows a per person variable fee of $50.00 per person.

- *Percentage of income.* With this method a percentage of total revenue is allocated to administrative fee cost recovery.
- *Integrated method.* This is a combination of the above methods. Exhibit 17 uses the integrated method. There is a fixed administrative fee of $3,000 plus a per person variable fee of $50.00.

There is no one correct method for recovering administrative fees. Each method can be appropriate, depending on the requirements of individual organizations. However, with all administrative cost-recovery methods it is important to establish (1) the total dollar amount of overhead that needs to be recovered for a fiscal year and (2) an appropriate way to prorate this cost recovery of overhead to individual programs.

Tip 101
Introduce a rough draft of the budget early in negotiations with other people.

When working with individual clients, planning committees, or other key stakeholders such as cosponsoring organizations, it is important to introduce a rough draft of a program budget early in discussions. This rough draft will usually be incomplete. However, it serves as a concrete document that will help everyone focus on the realities related to financial planning and management of a program.

This also helps people to focus on details of the program rather than simply discussing program generalities. Do not be disappointed if people tear the budget apart. That is the purpose of the first rough draft — to focus people's attention on the financial side of program planning — and that often brings spirited debate resulting in both strong agreement on some items and strong disagreement on other items. This is a natural and predictable part of the overall planning process.

Tip 102
It usually takes working through a number of revisions before you come up with a budget that meets all the needs of the program and also deals with the realities of excellent financial management.

For large, complex conferences or workshops, it is not unusual for the program planner to have to develop over a dozen versions of a budget before a final version meets the goals of the program and before agreement is reached with the key stakeholders on the dollar amount of the registration fee. This is a normal, expected part of the financial negotiation process.

Tip 103
Design an easy-to-use budget form.

There is no one form that can be used by everyone to plan all budgets. However, the form in Exhibit 17 is a prototype that can be modified to fit the needs of most meeting planners, whether you are planning small or large programs. When adapting this form for your own needs, the following five guidelines should be considered:

1. The form should be able to be used for all types of programs managed by your office. This allows the routine of budget planning to be simplified.
2. The form must always keep fixed and variable expenses separate. If this is not done, there is no way to figure an accurate break-even point.
3. If registrations can be charged to a credit card, the service fee for this option must be included as an expense item for all registrants.
4. An appropriate amount should always be added to cover miscellaneous expenses. As a general rule, at least 10 percent of all fixed costs should be added in this category. A higher percentage may be necessary, depending on the individual requirements of your program.
5. Complimentary expenses should always be figured as direct, fixed expenses. Complimentary expenses are calculated as the sum of all per person variable expenses times the number of complimentary registrations given.

These five guidelines have been incorporated into the budget form found in Exhibit 17.

Tip 104
Conduct a comprehensive budget wrap-up every thirty days for each program.

Individual program budgets need constant attention. Therefore, it is important to conduct a thorough budget wrap-up every thirty days for each separate program budget. This will enable you to (1) update your projections for income and expenses for each program in relation to your total year's budget, (2) review each budget to decide what income or expenses must still be posted to each account, and (3) catch errors that occur in all budgeting systems.

Tip 105
When using a budget planning form that has been programmed on an electronic spreadsheet, first learn how to do budget planning by hand.

Computer printouts look very official. In fact, they are so official-looking that people will tend to believe all the figures. If you first learn how to manage the budgeting process by hand, you will become aware of the assumptions behind each budget figure. This will make it easier to spot errors on computer printouts. Such errors are often caused by programming errors or errors in the assumptions behind figures. Therefore, be sure to learn how to figure a program budget by hand before relying on computers. This will ensure that you completely grasp all the budgeting principles. Then use computers to handle the mechanics of process quickly and efficiently.

Tip 106
Take into account what inflation can do to all program expenses.

When planning budgets, there is often a tendency to use today's prices for expense estimates. These may be reliable if the program takes place within the next several months. However, when planning large, complex programs, it is not unusual to have to plan a budget one to three years in advance. This presents some special problems when trying to estimate expenses.

Today's high rates of inflation hit every area of our economy. Six months from now people can expect to pay more for most things they purchase. In planning a program that will be held in the future, plan for inflation. Items that are affected most often by inflation are food, airline travel, mailing charges, and paper supplies. Do not use today's rates for planning expenses more than three months in advance unless you have a guarantee in writing that the same item or service will be available at a stated rate when the program is actually held. List in the budget the dollar amount you project to pay for something when you actually will have to pay the bill, not when you plan the budget.

Tip 107
Establish the necessary checks and balances to control expenditures.

It is important to clearly establish who has the authority to commit expenditures for any program. Neglecting to do this can be one of the easiest and fastest ways to overspend a budget, wind up in the hole, and create hard feelings for everyone involved. Avoid this by establishing clear control over any budget.

Specify during the beginning planning stages who is the official program administrator in charge of managing the budget. Make sure everyone understands that only this person can incur any expense. Do not wait until a problem develops to establish this authority over the budget. Instead, do this as a routine element of good budget planning before any problems develop.

Tip 108
Plan for decentralized accounting of all income and expenses.

If you are a private entrepreneur in business for yourself, this is usually not a problem. You will already have decentralized your accounting to your own office. However, if you are part of a larger organization — such as the conference office at a large university, a large professional association, or a large hospital — you probably are required to process all income and expenses through a central accounting office according to your parent organization's specific rules and regulations. When this happens, typically you will receive a printout of your account every thirty days. However, there is often a problem with this printout. It usually lags about thirty to ninety days behind reflecting the reality of what is happening related to the budgets of your individual programs.

Therefore, in order to have access to the most accurate information regarding each individual account, it is usually necessary to set up a separate, decentralized accounting process in your own office. Do this using an electronic spreadsheet or a relational data base on a personal computer. Then adopt the guideline that all income and all expenses will be posted to the appropriate account every twenty-four hours. In this way you will ensure that you can get an accurate printout of exactly where you stand in relation to each individual account, and this printout will be accurate within the last twenty-four hours to reflect your last posting.

Designing this type of decentralized accounting system that is accurate and easy to use will improve the quality of daily decision making related to financial management in your organization.

Tip 109
Create a printout that clearly identifies all income and expenses for each individual program.

Exhibit 19 shows an easy way to account for income and expenses related to each program.

Exhibit 19. Spreadsheet Summarizing Income and Expenses.

	A	B	C	D	E
1					
2					
3	Sample Electronic Spreadsheet Summarizing All Income and Expenses for a Single Program				
4					
5					
6	Income				
7		ID Number	Person	Amount	
8					
9		59455	Small, Martha	$325	
10		54645	Dresselhaus, Mark	$325	
11		69532	Leonard, Dee	$325	
12		69359	Flynn, Peggy	$325	
13		89537	Eversoll, Deanns	$325	
14		25632	Miller, Elmer	$325	
15		78793	Van Kekerix, Marv	$325	
16		89657	McMahon, Monty	$325	
17		54223	Elliott, Kim	$325	
18		36963	Bowmaster, William	$325	
19		72361	Abbott, Ruth	$325	
20		77771	Rathje, Kathleen	$325	
21		65101	Milligan, Sam	$325	
22		58401	Hammer, Larry	$325	
23		99930	Lester, Linda	$325	
24					
25			Total Income	$4,875	
26					

Exhibit 19. Spreadsheet Summarizing Income and Expenses, Cont'd.

	A	B	C	D	E	F	G
1							
2							
3	Expenses						
4		ID Number	Payee	Description	Amount	Paid	Encumbered
5							
6		56852	Union Catering Service	15 lunches @ 14	$210.23	√	
7		56831	Acme Printing	Programs	$125.36	√	
8		45863	Audiovisual Equipment	Slide projector rental	$55.00	√	√
9		56325	Wendaman's Trophy House	Awards	$245.17	√	
10		85641	Union	Brochure printing	$350.00	√	
11		56542	Marlene Sanders	Graphic design	$101.14		√
12		69352	Acme Printing	Mailing and handling charges	$427.98	√	
13		25321	Brian Foster	Photography	$75.00	√	
14		59632	Zaaap Typesetting	Typesetting	$147.23	√	
15		95328	Dunhill	List rental	$315.84		√
16		1590	Budget Transfer	Administrative fee	$2,500.00		
17							
18				Total	$4,552.95		
19							
20							
21	Budget Summary						
22							
23		Total Income		$4,875.00			
24		Total Expenses		$4,552.95			
25							
26		Balance		$322.05			

Note that identification numbers as well as the names of program registrants are included as a way of accounting for income. In the expense category, columns are included to indicate either that each expense item has been paid or that the bill will be arriving later but the exact money to pay the bill has been encumbered.

Tip 110
Establish a reliable encumbrance system.

Encumbrances are useful for budget reviews. Encumbering money means that you formally note an expense item, along with the exact amount of the expense, even though you may not actually have paid the bill. For example, at a workshop you may have had fifty lunches served by a hotel. Each lunch costs $14 including tax and gratuity. In order to accomplish a comprehensive budget review, you will need to include $50 \times \$14 = \$700$ on your review statement, even though you may not have actually received and paid the bill from the hotel. List this type of known expense in the encumbrance column on the printout in Exhibit 19. When the bill actually arrives and has been paid, move the check mark from the encumbrance column to the paid column.

Tip 111
Avoid the ten mistakes most often made in financial planning.

Avoiding these most often made mistakes is critical to overall leadership success for program planners. These ten major mistakes are as follows:

1. Developing financial planning systems that are so difficult to learn that staff actively resist learning them
2. Failing to institute a comprehensive accounting system that keeps track of all individual programs by separate accounts
3. Not establishing systems for accurately identifying all expenses and recovering these through income
4. Not planning a minimum of one year in advance for an accurate dollar amount for expenses that must be recovered through administrative fees charged to individual programs
5. Not making clear distinctions between fixed and variable expenses on all budgets
6. Not posting all income and expenses for each separate account, or program, each day
7. Not developing a comprehensive proposed budget for each program before any income is collected or any expenses are incurred
8. Not clearly establishing exactly who is in charge of managing each individual program budget
9. Not conducting a thorough review and update of all program accounts each month
10. Not teaching all staff members how to become expert financial planners

These mistakes can be avoided with careful, advance planning. Compare this list to your own procedures and make adjustments as necessary.

Summary

Good budget planning and management is not a magical or mystical process. Mostly it involves hard work, attention to detail, skill in negotiation, and establishing an effective record-keeping system that will give you (1) up-to-date information about any individual account or (2) a comprehensive wrap-up of all your program accounts so that you can see how effective you are in meeting your financial goals of breaking even for your entire operation.

The tips in this chapter have been distilled from the professional practice of professionals who plan conferences and workshops. Use the tips, adapt them, add to them, and develop your own checklists to ensure that your financial planning and management are of the same excellent level as your program management. When this happens, you will have positioned yourself and your organization to maximize success.

Exhibit 20. Budget Preparation Checklist.

The following checklist covers the major budget areas that are important to most program planners. This list, with the additions and revisions necessary to meet the needs of your organization, can serve as a guideline to use when planning budgets for any type of conference, institute, workshop, or meeting.

_____ 1. Always clearly distinguish between fixed and variable expenses on all budgets.

_____ 2. Estimate travel expenses for presenters as accurately as possible, based on best available data. Take into account the rise in prices between the time the budget is prepared and the time the expenses will actually be incurred. A travel agent can estimate the average projected monthly increases for air fares, for example.

_____ 3. Include fringe benefits and other appropriate expenses such as meals, parking, and miscellaneous expenses in the total expenses for program presenters.

_____ 4. Build in an appropriate administrative fee to recover office and other administrative expenses.

_____ 5. Include all expenses associated with direct mailing of brochures, including mailing service charges if a mailing house is used.

_____ 6. If the program is to be evaluated, include expenses for machine- or hand-tabulation of results.

_____ 7. Decide on audiovisual requirements and include these expenses.

_____ 8. Get accurate estimates for all food, including coffee breaks.

_____ 9. Add to all food expenses the appropriate percentage for tax and gratuity.

_____ 10. Include costs for duplicating all handouts such as programs, rosters, name tags, and workshop materials.

_____ 11. Include the service fee for credit card registration if you use this option.

_____ 12. Treat complimentary registrations as real, fixed expenses. Calculate them as the number of complimentary registrations times the sum total of the per person variable expenses.

_____ 13. Have at least one other person not involved in the preparation of the budget check it for accuracy. Everyone makes mistakes.

5

Negotiating
Favorable Contracts:

Seventeen Tips for
Securing Meeting Space,
Lodging, and Meals

The world of negotiating successful contracts for meeting space, lodging, and meals is complex and often confusing. There are many legal issues to be aware of and traps to avoid. In order to help you achieve the most favorable terms, this chapter contains actual sample contracts to illustrate what should and should not be included when booking meeting space, lodging, and meals for conferences and workshops. Many practical tips are discussed and analyzed to assist you in this special negotiating area so that you can develop the kind of contracts that are in the best interests of you, your organization, and its programs.

Tip 112
Choose an appropriate location for the program.

Choosing an appropriate location involves much more than just picking an appropriate physical facility. It involves consideration of the city, availability and appropriateness of leisure-time activities, costs for lodging and meals, and consideration of the image evoked in the minds of people regarding the location.

The following are three major issues to consider before deciding on the location for a program:

- Is the location appropriate to the major purpose of the program? For example, if the major goal of the program is to create an isolated en-

103

vironment in which forty people will lock themselves up for three days to develop a long-range plan to guide the future of their organization, a resort area in an isolated setting might be more appropriate than a large hotel in a major metropolitan area.

- If participants have to seek the approval of supervisors to attend, you may want to think twice before choosing a major vacation resort site for the program. An organization that is sensitive about its image does not want to appear to be financing staff vacations.

- If the sponsoring organization has a clearly articulated set of values, the location should complement these values and not work against them. For example, a major religious group probably would not want to choose Las Vegas for a youth leadership conference.

Choosing an appropriate program location can be an important part of developing an overall successful marketing strategy for any program. Locations should be chosen to enhance the goals of the program and be appropriate for the content as well as the image of the sponsoring organization.

Tip 113
Never schedule a program at a facility you have not visited recently.

The meeting facility business is an industry in which there is high staff turnover. Facilities are bought and sold quietly, and new management comes in while the old swiftly disappears. Today's "in" facility that provides excellent service can decline quickly. Chefs come and go. As a result, the quality of food and service can change dramatically within several weeks. Do not depend on ads in hotel and meeting facility guides as the key to booking space. Although such guides and other advertising are useful to help you select places you will consider, never book a program into a space that you or a staff member have not personally visited recently. Never! The risks are too great.

Tip 114
Avoid scheduling a program in a facility that is not yet open or that is undergoing major renovations.

Picture this. You have booked a program for 200 people into a reliable hotel that you have been pleased with in the past. The hotel is undergoing major renovations. As the sales manager noted when you signed the contract, "These renovations will enable us to serve you better." You were promised when you booked the space that the renovations would be finished eight weeks before your program takes place.

It is 8:45 A.M. and your program has just started. Suddenly, from next door comes the deafening sound of air hammers and electric saws. Your participants cannot hear the program presenter without straining. In short, the tone of your meeting environment has been sabotaged. You complain to the manager and are told that they regret the inconvenience but that the noise can't be helped. The manager says, "Our union rules are such that we cannot stagger work hours for people working on the renovations. We regret that we are behind in our schedule. It is the contractor's fault and there is nothing we can do about it. Please bear with us and accept our apologies for the inconvenience."

This is not an exaggerated horror story. It happens all the time in the conference and workshop business. Therefore, to avoid this, inquire before signing a contract whether or not any major renovations are going to be in progress while your program is there. If they are, pick another facility. Do not risk ruining the educational nature of your program with noise and inconvenience over which you will have no control.

The same rule holds true for selecting a site that is not open but that has promised to open by a certain date. The rule of thumb for the opening of commercial meeting facilities is that you can generally add six months to a year to the announced opening date. Do not book space into any facility that is not already opened and functioning in a superior fashion. You cannot risk the success of your program to things over which you have no control — such as construction delays due to weather, unions, scheduling, lawsuits, and disagreements over contracts.

Tip 115
Find out the range of conference rates at facilities in a community before booking any space.

It is rare in the business of planning conferences and workshops to be limited to only one choice for a place to hold a program. In most cases, while you may have special needs, you will find that a number of facilities in a community are suitable. Therefore, in order to negotiate from a position of strength, make inquiries about special conference rates before actually visiting the sales office at various facilities. Never accept the rate quoted initially unless you are convinced that it is the best rate possible. Most sales offices in meeting facilities have some leeway and, if pressed, will often give you lower rates than those initially quoted. To find out about the range of rates available, consider doing the following:

• Phone around to a number of facilities and ask for quotes on their special conference rates. Tell the sales representative that you have a limited amount of time and that you need a quote on the lowest conference rate available.

• Visit several of the facilities in which you are most interested. Look for a conference or meeting in progress. Introduce yourself to some of the participants in the lobby and ask what they are paying for conference rates for sleeping rooms. You can usually negotiate these same rates if they are more favorable than the ones initially quoted.

• Ask the facility for a list of six people who have held programs similar to yours recently. Call them for references. Find out what rates they were able to obtain, and also inquire about the quality of service provided by the facility.

It is important to keep in mind that the sales office in a meeting facility is in business to make a profit. Therefore, it is in their best interest to maximize their profits through charging you the highest possible rates. However, it is in your best interest to obtain the lowest possible rates. In order to do this, you will have to obtain reliable data so that you will know what your negotiating range is and when you will have to stop and agree to pay the rates quoted. However, without some good solid research to provide you with these ranges, you will be negotiating from a position of weakness instead of strength.

For example, recently a program planner was booking a conference into a large, prestigious hotel in a major convention city. During the meeting in the sales office, she was quoted rates of $105 per night single as the special conference rate, which the sales manager assured her was as low as they could go from their regular rate of $150 per night. Her attempts to negotiate a lower rate were rebuffed. She excused herself for a few minutes under the pretext of walking about the facility alone to "get a feeling for the place." During this time she stopped four people in the lobby who were checking out from a large, state-wide conference that had been there for three days. After introducing herself, she found that all of them were paying $80 per night for the special conference rate. Armed with that information, she returned to the sales office and offered to pay the same rate. The sales manager finally agreed because she indicated that even though she liked their facility very much, she was willing to take her business elsewhere in order to obtain more favorable rates.

Tip 116
Negotiate and sign a contract designed to meet your needs for meeting space, lodging, and food.

Do not depend on verbal agreements either in person or over the phone related to space, lodging, or food. Instead, work with a facility's sales representative until you both have agreed on conditions acceptable to your respective needs. Then have the sales representative draw up a contract in which everything is stated in writing. Exhibit 21 illustrates a typical sample contract for meeting space and lodging at a hotel. Food contracts are often negotiated separately. They will be covered later in the chapter.

Exhibit 21. Lodging and Meeting Space Contract.

Organization: Seminar Providers, Inc.

Address: 5837 W. 57th Street
New York, New York

Meeting Name: Statistical Quality Control for Manufacturing Systems
Engineers

Anticipated Attendance: 125

Contact: Sandra Exeter

Dates: March 3–6

Day:	Sunday	Monday	Tuesday	Wednesday
Date:	March 3	March 4	March 5	March 6
Rooms:	125	125	125	0

Guest Room Rates:

Rates for the above rooms will be $95 per single occupancy, $115 per double occupancy, and $20 per additional person, per room, per night. Applicable taxes will be added and these rates are net noncommissionable.

Pre-Arrivals/Stay-Overs

Guests arriving prior to or departing after the dates outlined will be confirmed on a space-available basis at this group rate.

Reservation Method

The hotel will supply, for your attendees, reservation cards that will be imprinted with the name of your organization, the dates, and the applicable rates. These cards need to be returned to our Reservation Department by February 3. We encourage you to ask your guests to make phone reservations since this provides faster service. We will acknowledge all reservations with a written confirmation.

Reservation Guarantee

Please note that our check-in time is 4:00 P.M., and our check-out time is 12 noon. Our bellpersons will assist you with any luggage storage needs. If guests plan to arrive after 6:00 P.M., they must guarantee their late arrival on their credit card. Otherwise their reservations will be canceled at 6:00 P.M. on the scheduled date of arrival.

Hospitality Suites

No suites are presently being held. Should you wish to reserve a suite, the rates range from $250 to $500 per day.

Food and Beverage

The hotel must purchase, prepare, and serve all food and beverages. Hotel policy does not allow food and beverages to be brought into the banquet facilities or hospitality suites. Your contract for meals is included as a separate agreement.

Exhibit 21. Lodging and Meeting Space Contract, Cont'd.

Meeting Space

We will provide you with a meeting room arranged classroom style to seat 125 people. This room has been reserved for March 4 and 5 from 8:00 A.M. until 10:00 P.M. On March 6, the meeting room is reserved from 8:00 A.M. until 1:00 P.M.

Audiovisual Equipment

Audiovisual equipment may be rented through the hotel sales office that acts as a booking agent for local audiovisual supply businesses. A list of audiovisual equipment you will require should be given to the sales office one week before the beginning of the event.

Billing

It is our understanding that each individual will be responsible for all room and incidental charges.

Please find enclosed a direct billing form for your completion. This information is required to establish a master account for your program for such items as food and other expenses agreed to.

The undersigned agrees to make immediate payment upon receipt of our statement. In the event that payment is not made within thirty (30) days, it is agreed that the hotel may impose a 1½ % monthly late payment fee, or the maximum allowed by law, on the unpaid balance and the reasonable cost of collection, including attorneys' fees.

Cancellation Clause

In the event that your program is canceled for any reason 120 or more days before the event, you agree to make immediate payment to the hotel for the total cost of rooms reserved for the first night, plus 50 percent of the expenses for rooms reserved for all subsequent nights. This is calculated as follows:

First night	125 rooms × $95 = $11,875.00	
Second night	125 rooms × $95 = $11,875 minus	
	50% =	5,937.00
Third night	Same	5,937.00
	Total	$23,749.00

In the event that your program is canceled for any reason less than 120 days before the first day of the event, you agree to pay the hotel the full cost for all reserved rooms. This is calculated as 125 rooms × $95 per room × 3 nights = $33,625.00.

Deposit

A deposit of $5,000 is required to complete this contract. This deposit must be made within thirty (30) days of signing this confirmation and agreement in order to hold your space. The deposit will be applied to your final bill.

Impossibility

Should events beyond either party's control, such as strikes, acts of God, or civil disturbance, materially affect either party's ability to perform, this agreement shall be terminated without penalty to either party.

Arbitration

Arbitration shall be conditioned precedent to any right of legal action. Any controversy or claims arising out of or relating to this contract, or breach thereof, shall be settled by ar-

Exhibit 21. Lodging and Meeting Space Contract, Cont'd.

bitration in accordance with the Commercial Arbitration Rules of the American Arbitration Association, and any judgment upon the award rendered by the arbitrator may be entered in any court having jurisdiction thereof.

Acceptance

Enclosed with the Confirmation and Agreement is a duplicate copy of same. If the items outlined meet with your approval, please sign and return within two weeks.

Accepted and Agreed to: Accepted and Agreed to:
The Remarque West Hotel

_____   _____
Marlin Fox   Sandra Exeter
Director of Sales   Director of Programs
                                                Seminar Providers, Inc.

_____   _____
(Date)   (Date)

Source: Planning and Marketing Conferences and Workshops: Tips, Tools, and Techniques, by Robert G. Simerly. San Francisco: Jossey-Bass. Copyright ©1990. Permission granted to reproduce.

Exhibit 21 represents a typical contract generated by providers of meeting facilities. The conditions of the contract, however, are much more favorably balanced in favor of the hotel, to the disadvantage of the client. The next tips analyze this issue in detail and provide advice on how you can rewrite the contract with terms more favorable to you as the client.

Tip 117
If a provider of facilities presents you with a draft of a contract that is not in your best interest, carefully negotiate changes before signing it.

In any negotiation process, people drafting the initial version of a contract usually create ideal conditions and guarantees for their organization. Therefore, do not be surprised if the first draft of a suggested contract with a facility has a number of clauses that are unfavorable for you and your organization. Remember the first rule of contracts—a document is never a contract until all parties have agreed to all the terms.

If there are items in the contract that are not in your best interests, negotiate changes. For example, Exhibit 22 illustrates a different version of the contract presented in Exhibit 21.

Exhibit 22. Revised Hotel and Meeting Space Contract.

Confirmation and Agreement

Organization: Seminar Providers, Inc.

Address: 5837 W. 57th Street
New York, New York

Meeting Name: Statistical Quality Control for Manufacturing Systems Engineers

Anticipated Attendance: 125

Contact: Sandra Exeter

Dates: March 3–6

Day:	Sunday	Monday	Tuesday	Wednesday
Date:	March 3	March 4	March 5	March 6
Rooms:	125	125	125	0

Guest Room Rates:

Rates for the above rooms will be $95 per single occupancy, $115 per double occupancy, and $20 per additional person, per room, per night. Applicable taxes will be added and these rates are net noncommmissionable.

Pre-Arrivals/Stay-Overs

Guests arriving prior to or departing after the dates outlined will be confirmed on a space-available basis at this group rate.

Reservation Method

The hotel will supply, for your attendees, reservation cards which will be imprinted with the name of your organization, the dates, and the applicable rates. These cards need to be returned to our Reservation Department by February 3. We encourage you to ask your guests to make phone reservations since this provides faster service. We will acknowledge all reservations with a written confirmation.

Reservation Guarantee

Please note that our check-in time is 4:00 P.M., and our check-out time is 12 noon. Our bellpersons will assist you with any luggage storage needs. If guests plan to arrive after 6:00 P.M., they must guarantee their late arrival on their credit card. Otherwise the reservations will be canceled at 6:00 P.M. on the scheduled date of arrival.

Hospitality Suites

No suites are presently being held. Should you wish to reserve a suite, the rates range from $250 to $500 per day.

Food and Beverage

The hotel must purchase, prepare, and serve all food and beverages. Hotel policy does not allow food and beverages to be brought into the banquet facilities or hospitality suites. Your contract for meals is included as a separate agreement.

Exhibit 22. Revised Hotel and Meeting Space Contract, Cont'd.

Meeting Space

We will provide you with a meeting room arranged classroom style to seat 125 people. This room has been reserved for March 4 and 5 from 8:00 A.M. to 10:00 P.M. On March 6, the meeting room is reserved from 8:00 A.M. until 1:00 P.M.

Audiovisual Equipment

Audiovisual equipment may be rented through the hotel sales office that acts as a broker for local audiovisual supply businesses. A list of audiovisual equipment you require should be given to the sales office one week before the beginning of your event.

Billing

It is our understanding that each individual guest will be responsible for all room and incidental charges.

Please find enclosed a direct billing form for your completion. This information is required to establish a master account for your program for such items as food and other expenses agreed to.

The undersigned agrees to make immediate payment upon receipt of our statement. In the event that payment is not made within thirty (30) days, it is agreed that the hotel may impose a 1½% monthly late payment fee, or the maximum allowed by law, on the unpaid balance and the reasonable cost of collection, including attorneys' fees.

Cancellation Clause

It is agreed that all parties to this contract are acting in good faith in estimating the number of rooms to be reserved. The block of 125 rooms will be held until thirty days (30 days) before the program. At that time, any unreserved rooms will be released for sale to the general public.

Any conference guests desiring rooms from that point on will still be able to take advantage of the special conference rate if rooms are available. However, the availability of these rooms cannot be guaranteed.

Acceptance

Enclosed with the Confirmation and Agreement is a duplicate copy of same. If the items outlined meet with your approval, please sign and return it within two weeks. This signed contract will serve as our mutual confirmation of the terms outlined therein.

Accepted and Agreed to: Accepted and Agreed to:
The Remarque West Hotel

_____   _____
Marlin Fox   Sandra Exeter
Director of Sales   Director of Program
                                           Seminar Providers, Inc.

_____   _____
(Date)   (Date)

This time, however, the sponsoring organization has negotiated a number of major changes. Among these are the following:

• The arbitration clause has been removed. Do not fall into the trap of signing a hotel contract in which you agree in advance how differences of opinion will be handled if a dispute arises. Unless you have a different agreement, the usual due process in the courts will be used if differences cannot be resolved through informal discussions. Do not give up your right to sue, using due process, in the event of disagreements. When you sign an arbitration clause, you give up this right. Arbitration clauses are almost always unfavorable for you as a client.

• The deposit clause requiring a $5,000 deposit has been eliminated. Think twice about depositing money as part of your contract. For one thing, the hotel will have your money and earn interest on it until the event takes place. For another, in case of a dispute they will be holding a large amount of your money. This will put you at a major disadvantage in any subsequent negotiations.

• The impossibility clause has been eliminated. In the unlikely event that problems do arise in this area, not having a previous agreement related to this leaves open a wider range of options to resolving the problem.

• The cancellation policy has been completely reworded. The new wording reflects a good-faith working relationship and acknowledges the reality of the financial risks inherent in planning conferences and workshops. If the program does have to be canceled because enough people did not register, there will be no penalty to you.

• The cancellation policy clause has been completely reworded so that it enables the hotel to release any of the unsold rooms booked by you thirty days before the program. This is a fair and reasonable clause because it gives the hotel a chance to sell these rooms to the general public on a first-come, first-served basis. It is not reasonable to expect a hotel to hold unreserved rooms for less than 30 days before the event unless you are willing to guarantee payment.

The contract in Exhibit 22 has much more favorable terms for you as the program planner. In essence, the contract in Exhibit 22 recognizes that planning conferences and workshops is a business with an element of risk. For example, you could conduct an extensive direct-mail advertising campaign and find that only a few people register. As a result, you must cancel in order to avoid losing a lot of money. The contract in Exhibit 22 gives you this option without having to pay the hotel a penalty.

Thus, the revised contract in Exhibit 22 is a business contract in which you and the hotel enter into a shared-risk agreement. Each of you plans in good faith, hoping that the number of registrations materializes. The hotel agrees to hold the block of rooms until thirty days before the event. After that date, the rooms are released for sale to the general public. People registering for the workshop after the thirty-day cutoff date may still secure the special conference rate. However, the hotel does not guarantee that rooms will be available. This shared-risk arrangement is the most commonly used contractual arrangement in the conference business today. However, many hotels and other types of meeting facilities will initially suggest very different terms — terms that are advantageous only to them and leave you assuming all the risk.

Tip 118
Negotiate complimentary rooms.

It is a common practice for program planners to negotiate for extra services or amenities. For example, it is customary for a hotel to give you a complimentary room for every fifty rooms sold each night. Therefore, for a program where 100 guests spend the night, you can usually negotiate two complimentary rooms. Make these available to program presenters or staff. This will help reduce your overall expenses. Be sure to have this agreement written into your contract.

Tip 119
Negotiate additional complimentary services.

These negotiations are most successful in such small but important areas as providing complimentary hospitality baskets in the rooms of VIPs. Typically these baskets contain fruit, cheeses, wine, desserts, and other snacks. If you have a small number of VIPs, it is reasonable to expect this additional service for any program that books fifty sleeping rooms a night. If your participant list is smaller or if your VIP list is large, you can easily make arrangements to pay for such hospitality baskets to be put in the rooms of all guests for a modest cost. Be sure to have any such agreements stated clearly in your contract.

Tip 120
If you have any doubts about a contract, consult an attorney.

Most contracts for lodging, meeting space, and meals are straightforward. As a result, if the terms are clear and you agree with them, it is usually not necessary to consult an attorney. However, if you have any doubts, do not sign the contract without obtaining good legal advice. The time and expense required to do this can save you headaches in the long run.

Tip 121
Remember, no contract is a contract until all parties agree to the terms.

Often the sales office in large hotels will inform program planners that they have a standard meeting contract similar to the one in Exhibit 21. The impression they will often convey is that the contract is carved in stone and that no terms in it can be altered. This impression is reinforced through preprinted documents that look very official. However, do not fall into the trap of thinking that any of these terms — such as cancellation clauses, arbitration clauses, and deposit required — cannot be changed. Also, be aware that it sometimes takes three or four drafts of a contract before all parties can agree to all the wording. This is a natural part of the negotiation process.

If you cannot negotiate terms that are satisfactory to you, shop around for a facility that is willing to meet your needs. However, you will find that almost all major facilities will modify their "standard contract" when they see that you are knowledgeable about contracts and are willing to take your business elsewhere if you cannot negotiate terms that are favorable to you and the needs of your program.

Tip 122
When negotiating a change in clauses of hotel contracts, always negotiate from a position of strength through assertiveness.

When you are negotiating with the hotel sales representative on the wording of the various clauses that will go into the written contract, always take the lead in asserting what you need for your program. For example, never begin by asking, "What is your hotel's cancellation policy?" This places you in a position of negotiating from weakness by assuming that there is a definite policy in the first place. Therefore, if they state a cancellation policy and you insist on changing the terms, the hotel sales representative is placed in the position of having to back down from their original position. This act of giving in does not help the negotiation process for either party.

Instead say, "We need to clarify up front the wording in the cancellation clause for the contract. I regret that my organization is not able to enter into a cancellation guarantee. Our fiscal policies do not allow us to pay for services not rendered. Instead, both of us need to recognize that we are entering into a shared-risk contract. Naturally, we will do everything possible to make our program a success. However, in the unlikely event that we cancel, we need the standard clause that we can cancel without penalty. And, naturally, we recognize that you are running a business, so we can feel comfortable including the usual clause that you will hold the block of rooms until thirty days before the event. At that time, any unreserved rooms will be released for sale to the general public."

If the hotel cannot accept these terms, you have two choices: (1) accept their terms, realizing that you are placing yourself at risk to lose what could possibly be a large sum of money in the event of cancellation, or (2) take your business elsewhere. In almost every case, the latter option is the best one from your point of view. Experience has proved that most hotel facilities will negotiate terms favorable to you as soon as they realize that you are knowledgeable about the complexities of hotel contracts and that you are willing to walk out the door of the sales office in order to secure space somewhere else with the terms you need.

Tip 123
If you are having a very large conference that will tie up the entire hotel facility for several days, you will probably have to negotiate a different type of cancellation clause.

The guidelines for cancellation policies thus far have been for smaller programs that do not tie up an entire meeting facility for several days. However, if you are negotiating a contract for a very large program that will require all the hotel's rooms for several days, it is not always possible to secure such a lenient cancellation policy, particularly at large, popular facilities during high season in major resort areas.

For example, suppose a hotel has 537 rooms and you are booking a large conference for three days that will require all 537 of these rooms. The conference is to be held three years away. Since cancellation of such a large conference could ruin a hotel's ability to sell this large block of space, you can expect to encounter a much more stringent cancellation agreement. Under such conditions, most hotels require a sliding scale payment if a program is canceled. Here are the typical terms they might suggest:

- Cancellation from the time the contract is signed until twelve months before the event — payment of 25 percent per night for all sleeping rooms booked
- Cancellation from the time the contract is signed until six months before the event — payment of 50 percent per night for all sleeping rooms booked
- Cancellation from the time the contract is signed until three months before the event — payment of 75 percent per night for all sleeping rooms booked
- Cancellation sooner than three months before the event — payment of 100 percent per night for all sleeping rooms booked

The reason why some hotels will often not negotiate more favorable cancellation agreements for such large programs that tie up their entire facilities is that these programs tend to be large conferences sponsored by businesses and professional associations. Often the officers and managers of these businesses and associations change from the time the contract is signed until the event takes place. As a result, if such a contract were not in place, organizations might have a new set of managers and officers come on board who, for some reason, would like to have the program at a different location. If a contract without stiff cancellation penalties were not in place, the hotel would be left to cope with the whims of this new planning committee or new group of officers.

It is not unusual for large conferences and conventions to book five to eight years in advance. The key players can change in this period of time. Such a cancellation clause protects the hotel from the vagaries and whims of new staff in an organization.

Tip 124
Negotiate a written contract for all meal functions.

Depending on the demands of your program and the requirements of the facility, you may or may not negotiate the food contract at the same time as the lodging contract. Whichever method you use, be sure to get all agreements in writing and have all key parties sign off on the agreement. Exhibit 23 shows a sample meal contract for the meeting described in the hotel contract in Exhibits 21 and 22.

Exhibit 23. Food Contract.

Organization: Seminar Providers, Inc.

Address: 5837 W. 57th Street
        New York, New York

Meeting Name: Statistical Quality Control for Mechanical Systems Engineers

Anticipated Attendance: 125

Contact: Sandra Exeter

This contract describes the meal functions to be arranged for the program named above:

Continental breakfast, March 3, served 8–9 A.M.
    (Juice, coffee, tea, and a variety of rolls)
    Cost: $6.50 per person

Coffee break, March 3, served 10:15–10:45 A.M.
    (Coffee and tea)
    Cost: $3.00 per person

Lunch, March 3, served 12 noon–1:30 P.M.
    (Soup, seafood salad, dessert, and beverage)
    Cost: $17.98 per person

Afternoon break, March 3, served 2:30–3:00 P.M.
    (Coffee, tea, juice, and soft drinks)
    Cost: $3.00 per person

Continental breakfast, March 4, served 8–9 A.M.
    (Juice, coffee, tea, and a variety of rolls)
    Cost: $6.50 per person

Coffee break, March 4, served 10:15–10:45 A.M.
    (Coffee and tea)
    Cost: $3.00 per person

Afternoon break, March 4, 2:30–3:00 P.M.
    (Coffee, tea, juice, and soft drinks)
    Cost: $3.00 per person

Continental breakfast, March 5, served 8–9 A.M.
    (Juice, coffee, tea, and a variety of rolls)
    Cost: $6.50 per person

Afternoon break, March 5, served 2:30–3:00 P.M.
    (Coffee, tea, juice, and soft drinks)
    Cost: $3.00 per person

Dinner, March 5, served 7–9 P.M.
    (Soup, salad, prime rib, baked potato, vegetable, dessert, beverages, and wine)
    Cost: $28.98 per person

Continental breakfast, March 6, served 8–9 A.M.
    (Coffee, tea, juice, and a variety of rolls)
    Cost: $6.50 per person

Exhibit 23. Food Contract, Cont'd.

Taxes

All food prices plus applicable taxes (currently 10 percent)

Gratuity

A gratuity of 18 percent will be added to all food bills.

Guarantees

It is agreed that the sponsor will provide the hotel with a guarantee for number of meals and breaks a minimum of forty-eight hours before each scheduled event. Your guarantee may vary by 5 percent in either direction without penalty.

Acceptance

Enclosed are two copies of this agreement for food. If the items outlined meet with your approval, please sign and return it to me within two weeks.

Accepted and Agreed to: The Remarque West Hotel James Martin, Food Service Manager	Sandra Exeter Director of Programs Seminar Providers, Inc.
(Date)	(Date)

Source: Planning and Marketing Conferences and Workshops: Tips, Tools, and Techniques, by Robert G. Simerly. San Francisco: Jossey-Bass. Copyright ©1990. Permission granted to reproduce.

Tip 125
If you are dealing with upscale corporate executives, consider booking a block of rooms on the executive club floor of a hotel.

Increasingly, large, upscale hotels have several floors called their executive club floors. Entrance to these club floors is controlled by a special key that fits into the control panel inside the elevator. Thus, the general public does not have access to these special club floors.

The advantages of the club floors are that they usually have upscale rooms plus a wide range of services. For example, most club floors have a lounge with complimentary coffee, drinks, and food. At breakfast, they serve a continental breakfast or buffet so guests can avoid the breakfast lines in the regular restaurants. In the evenings they usually serve complimentary drinks and hors d'oeuvres. In addition, they usually offer newspapers, magazines, secretarial assistance, copy machines, FAX facilities, a concierge, and other amenities used by busy executives.

The rooms on these club floors cost more than regular rooms, even for conference rates. However, if you are dealing with an upscale executive development program where the registration fees and expenses are paid for by the participants' organization, this additional cost is usually not a problem. This extra service can go a long way toward creating a special ambience for your program.

Tip 126
When working with food service personnel to plan meals and social events, ask them to bring their best creativity to your food service.

The catering departments at most meeting facilities have standard, printed catering menus. These are useful in providing you with price ranges for food service. However, the standard catering menu often does not take into account your special needs, nor does it always reflect the highly creative approach food service personnel can bring to meal preparations when they feel that their professional opinion is highly valued.

Therefore, consider this as an approach for your next event. After scanning price ranges from the printed catering menu and comparing these to what you can afford in your budget, say to the catering manager, "All of this sounds excellent. However, I also want to ensure that your staff bring their own individuality and creativity to the preparations for our event. Therefore, based on your expertise and your understanding of our entire conference and its audience, what would you recommend that will make both you and us look like we have taken very special care in making this a special event for our participants?"

If you are working with a catering sales manager, ask to speak to the head chef. Seek recommendations from both of these people. It is important to establish this personal rapport with both the catering manager and the chef. This begins to create the psychological contract among you that becomes a bond emphasizing excellence. You have signaled that you very much want something other than their routine service. You are communicating that you value their professional experience. When this approach is used, it almost always results in an unparalleled standard of excellence in food service.

A good way to establish what you are asking for is to say, "If you were preparing this event for a professional group of your peers, what would you recommend that would be special and make all of us look excellent?" Conclude with, "As you consider this request, we want you to bring your most creative thinking to your recommendations."

As your discussions evolve, emphasize the fact that your group will appreciate not only excellent food preparation but also excellent presentation. Discuss the tone and level of service you expect from the servers. Emphasize how important this quality of service is to the overall success of your program.

Conversations such as this usually establish a unique relationship between you and the food service office. As a result, they will see your event as something special in their daily routine of providing food service to a wide variety of groups. Suddenly you move from being a routine customer to a valued client, colleague, and friend. Thus, your event becomes as special to the food service staff as it is to you. Taking time to establish this personal relationship in which you indicate you place high value on the staff's creativity, individuality, and excellence will usually pay big dividends in the form of quality service.

Tip 127
When selecting food, carefully determine the expectations of your audience as well as the type of program you have planned. Consider avoiding heavier foods in favor of lighter ones, and larger portions in favor of smaller ones.

The type and amount of food to be served at a program can be a tricky issue. Americans' food tastes have undergone dramatic changes within the last few years. Instead of large, all-you-can-eat meals we are moving toward eating patterns based on "grazing." Many people tend to eat several snacks throughout the day, with less food at each meal and less time spent in food consumption. To illustrate this fact, consider the popularity of food centers in shopping malls where you can pick from a wide variety of well-prepared foods served in modest portions, in a manner that enables you to grab a bite, relax, and then be on your way. In many areas of the country, this is in sharp contrast to former eating patterns that emphasized full-service restaurants serving large portions in a leisurely fashion.

Therefore, when planning meal events, consider carefully the following:

* What is the makeup of your audience?
* What expectations will they have for meals?
* Are they food connoisseurs or basic meat-and-potatoes people?
* What follows a meal—speeches, workshops, formal presentations, or leisure time?

Consider the following guidelines before making final decisions:

- Because people are much more conscious about calories and their health, many groups prefer lighter, weight-conscious meals — especially for lunch.
- Heavier meals encourage people to doze off afterwards. Therefore, if you have a program following a meal, it becomes especially important to consider ordering lighter food.
- Many people have come to expect lighter lunches, even if they prefer heavier dinners. Therefore, for lunch consider fruit plates, quiche, soup, sandwiches, salads, or light entrees. Consider eliminating dessert entirely or having a light dessert such as fruit or sherbet.

Above all, consider the composition of your audience and the expectations they have for the kind of food to be served. The following examples illustrate the importance of this:

- A group of 400 professional home economists held a national conference at a large university conference facility. Because being concerned with nutrition was part of the makeup of the daily lives of this professional group, their program planners requested light, nutritious meals. They even printed on the menu at each table the calorie and cholesterol count for each item served. The evaluations indicated that the group appreciated this extra attention to the nutritional content of meals. They were especially complimentary of the printing of the calorie and cholesterol count on the menus.

- A group of highway engineers held an annual conference of 900 people each year at a large hotel. The group was almost entirely male, the average age was fifty-five, and the group was a regional group from the Midwest who usually worked outdoors and ate hearty lunches to provide energy for hard physical labor in the afternoon. In an attempt to introduce them to new experiences, one year they were served chef salads for lunch followed by sherbet. The next day they were served quiche and salad with fruit for dessert. On the evaluations the participants complained loudly about the poor food. As many noted, "There wasn't even enough to fill you up!"

The next year the conference planners returned to a more traditional menu — soup followed by a large salad. The entree was large cuts of prime rib with baked potatoes, butter, and sour cream. Green beans were served on the side. Dessert was a large serving of strawberry shortcake with whipped cream. The evaluations this time were very different. Everyone raved about the excellent food. A number of people even mentioned that it was "much better than last year."

- A group of 200 high school students attended a one-week leadership workshop at a local university. They were served formal, sit-down lunches and dinners. The evaluations showed that the group was not particularly pleased with the meals. The next year the meeting planners set up outdoor food stations on the lawn for lunch and dinner. During the course of the week they provided such items as hot dogs, hamburgers, sandwiches, and pizza, along with a dessert bar that enabled students to make their own ice cream sundaes. The evaluations for the food were excellent. When interviewed, a number of students mentioned that they liked to roam around and talk to their friends or that they enjoyed sitting on the grass in informal groups.

• A group of 150 continuing educators held a regional conference at Jackson Hole, Wyoming. For one of the meals the conference planners staged an outdoor cookout of buffalo burgers. The evaluations showed that this was a very popular meal because for most of the group eating buffalo meat was a unique event. In addition, the meal was very nutritious because buffalo meat is very lean. The group was mature and adventuresome and enjoyed trying new things, so they viewed this as a special treat.

In summary, it is important to meet the expectations of the group when planning meals. Satisfaction with food spills over into all other aspects of the program. Therefore, it is important to give considerable attention to the content of meals in addition to the service.

Tip 128
Be prepared to pay a fair market price for the quality of food and service you desire.

Most planners of conferences and workshops and catering managers at conference facilities have the same goal—to offer quality service. If this is what you want, do not expect the catering department to provide top-quality food and service at rock-bottom prices. These two expectations are incompatible.

Therefore, before making your final decisions about food service, do some comparison shopping in the city where you are holding your event. This will give you a good idea of price ranges for meal service in the facilities you are considering. For example, in large cities such as New York, Washington, D.C., Chicago, and New Orleans, you will probably be quoted much higher prices for meals than in small cities in the South or Midwest. One of the reasons for this is that food service staffs in larger cities and meeting facilities are usually unionized and therefore command higher salaries. In addition, the conference facilities in these larger cities have much higher operating costs for maintenance, real estate taxes, utilities, and other support services. These additional costs are passed on to you, the customer.

Meeting facilities are businesses and as such they are set up to produce profits for their investors. Therefore, be prepared to pay a fair market price for the value you want. Do not expect catering departments to lower prices because of the type of organization or group you represent. When negotiating prices for food service, the old adage is true—you usually get exactly what you pay for. Of course, once you have entered into an agreement, you have every right to expect excellence in food preparation, presentation, and service.

Summary

This chapter has presented a wide variety of tips for successfully negotiating contracts for meeting, lodging, and food. In order to avoid misunderstandings later, all agreements for these items should be in writing. It has been emphasized that no contract is a contract until all parties involved have agreed to the terms. Therefore, if a meeting facility presents you with an initial contract that is not advantageous to your needs, negotiate changes. If you cannot negotiate the kinds of changes you need, you will either have to accept their terms or take your business elsewhere. The last option is usually the most viable one, since most facilities can be flexible and arrange a contract to meet your specific needs. Therefore, be sure to do your homework and shop for comparable facilities and prices before making your final decision. In this way, you can be assured that through your negotiations you have developed the best set of arrangements for you, your organization, and your programs.

Exhibit 24. Checklist for Negotiating Successful Contracts for Meeting Space, Lodging, and Meals.

Since negotiating favorable terms for meeting space, lodging, and meals is such a detailed, complex process, the following checklist serves as a reminder of major issues, principles, and guidelines to keep in mind during your negotiations. Use this checklist, with your own modifications, each time you negotiate with a hotel or other provider of space or food.

_____ 1. Check the location to make sure it is appropriate to the goals and image of your program.

_____ 2. Visit the meeting facility and walk through the space you will be using to determine its suitability.

_____ 3. Check to be sure that the facility will not be undergoing renovations during your meeting.

_____ 4. Get quotes on rates from other meeting facilities to ensure the most competitive price.

_____ 5. Carefully check all contracts for food and lodging to ensure that all terms are favorable to you.

_____ 6. Pay particular attention to cancellation clauses in contracts, making sure they are acceptable to you.

_____ 7. Remember, nothing is a contract until all parties have agreed to the terms. Negotiation is appropriate and expected.

_____ 8. Pay particular attention to clauses requiring you to agree in advance to use arbitration to settle any disputes. These are usually not in your best interests and should generally be negotiated out of any contract.

_____ 9. Pay particular attention to clauses requiring you to deposit money in advance. This rarely works to your advantage and can usually be negotiated out of most contracts.

_____ 10. Get reliable legal advice related to all your contracts.

_____ 11. The industry standard is for you to receive one complimentary room for every fifty paid for each night.

_____ 12. Consider negotiating free room upgrades for VIPs.

_____ 13. Consider reserving rooms on the club floor of a hotel for corporate meetings involving executives.

_____ 14. Consider asking the catering department to suggest special theme meals rather than restricting yourself to the regular printed banquet menus.

_____ 15. Carefully consider the expectations of your audience when planning meals.

_____ 16. Be prepared to pay a fair market dollar for quality food and service.

Source: *Planning and Marketing Conferences and Workshops: Tips, Tools, and Techniques,* by Robert G. Simerly. San Francisco: Jossey-Bass. Copyright ©1990. Permission granted to reproduce.

6

Evaluating and
Improving Programs:

Eighteen Tips for
Determining Whether Programs
Are Achieving Goals
and Expectations

Designing successful program evaluations is an integral part of the total planning process for conferences and workshops. Evaluation is a complex issue, but the practical tips provided in this chapter demonstrate a wide variety of ways to design successful evaluations. The chapter emphasizes three major ideas. First, evaluation should be done in relation to clearly established program goals. Second, in order to be as effective as possible, evaluation instruments should be short so that people can complete them quickly. Longer evaluation instruments usually decrease your response rate and thus the validity of your findings. Third, evaluation needs to be reported and interpreted in relation to future program improvement.

Throughout this chapter the emphasis is on practical, easy-to-implement suggestions. Seven different evaluation instruments are presented to illustrate the principles discussed. These instruments can easily be adapted to meet the needs of your specific programs. The ultimate goal of all program evaluation is to provide information about how well the component parts of the program were received and to suggest ways to improve future programs.

Tip 129
Clearly distinguish between formative and summative evaluation.

The literature on evaluation is extensive. Basically, however, there are two different types of evaluation—formative and summative. Formative evaluation is evaluation that is done before and during a program. The purpose of formative evaluation is to help formulate ideas that improve all aspects of the program. For example, as part of planning a program on legal issues in personnel management, you might ask personnel directors to list the major legal issues they face in personnel management. This is formative evaluation. You are using these data to help design or implement a program.

Summative evaluation, however, is very different. Summative evaluation takes place at the end of a program. Its purpose is to summarize the reactions participants have to the program. It is these summative data that are used to make judgments about program success as well as about program changes for the future.

Therefore, when considering evaluation, it is important to plan for both formative and summative evaluation.

Tip 130
When using formative evaluation, interviews can be useful for collecting data.

A typical way to use formative evaluation effectively is to interview people regarding what they would like to see included in a program you are planning. For example, personnel directors in business could be asked to list their major legal problems in personnel administration as a way of determining what should be included in a program on that topic. This type of interviewing usually yields a wealth of rich, reliable data. In order to obtain these data, it is important to conduct these interviews according to a structured interview formula so that the same type of data is collected from each interviewee. This will yield the most valid results.

Interviews may be done in person or over the phone. Exhibit 25 illustrates a structured interview format that can easily be adapted to meet the formative evaluation needs of almost any program you are planning.

**Exhibit 25. Formative Interview Format for a Proposed
Two-Day Workshop Entitled "How Managers Can Avoid
Lawsuits Related to Personnel Management."**

We are thinking of planning a two-day workshop entitled "How Managers Can Avoid Lawsuits Related to Personnel Management." As part of our market research, we are surveying personnel managers in a wide variety of organizations to identify their major problems related to personnel management and the law. Specifically, the goal of our proposed program is to provide managers with an intensive update on legal issues so they can avoid lawsuits for themselves and their organizations.

Issue Identification

What are the five most important personnel management issues you face that have legal ramifications for you and your organization?

1.

2.

3.

4.

5.

Suggested Presenters

Do you know of any presenters you have heard recently who are particularly effective in dealing with this topic?

About the Beginning Manager

Beginning managers are often unaware of the legal implications of their actions in relation to a wide variety of personnel issues. Could you please list the five most critical mistakes you see beginning managers making in relation to legal issues of personnel management.

1.

2.

3.

4.

5.

Exhibit 25. Formative Interview Format for a Proposed Two-Day Workshop Entitled "How Managers Can Avoid Lawsuits Related to Personnel Management," Cont'd.

Other Suggestions

As you consider this very important topic, do you have any other suggestions for content to be covered in a two-day workshop?

Market Research

Would your organization be interested in sending managers to such a workshop?

_____ Definitely
_____ Probably
_____ Possibly
_____ Probably not
_____ Unsure

If your organization would be interested in sending managers to such a workshop, what days of the week would be most convenient for a workshop?

How long should such a workshop last?

What months would be most convenient?

What days of the month are most convenient?

Would your organization pay for the registration fee for people attending?

_____ Yes   _____ No   _____ Undecided

What would you consider to be a fair registration fee for your managers to pay for a two-day workshop on this topic?

Additional Comments

**Exhibit 25. Formative Interview Format for a Proposed
Two-Day Workshop Entitled "How Managers Can Avoid
Lawsuits Related to Personnel Management," Cont'd.**

Thanks!

Thanks so much for your assistance in reacting to our ideas. We appreciate your willingness to help us conduct market research for this very important topic. If we do proceed with planning such a program and you would like to be put on the mailing list to receive an announcement, just write your name, title, and mailing address below:

Name _____

Job title _____

Address _____

_____

_____

City _____ State _____ Zip _____

Note: This interview format can be adapted and used with personal interviews and telephone interviews as well as with written questionnaires.

Another example of the effective use of formative evaluation is the following: At a week-long executive development program, the program agenda was set for the first four days. As a result of interviews and discussions with participants, the program for the fifth day was not determined until the evening of the fourth day. The presenters created the agenda for the fifth day to meet specific needs expressed by participants. As a result, a series of three mini-workshops was created to address specific skill areas participants indicated they needed. These workshops were in the area of conflict management, time management, and working with the media to create effective public relations. Thus, data from evaluation conducted during the middle of the program were used to form the program for the last day.

Tip 131
Collect quantitative and qualitative data on evaluations.

Quantitative evaluation refers to anything that can easily be counted, classified, and categorized. For example, the following rating scale is an example of collecting quantitative data:

How do you rate the overall effectiveness of Sandra Wilson as the main workshop presenter?

1	2	3	4	5
Poor	Below average	Average	Above average	Very good

Ratings on this scale can be counted. Averages can be calculated. Data are easy to report.

Qualitative data, however, are harder to count, code, and report because they ask respondents to write their reactions without listing them on a numerical scale. For example, the following evaluation question asks for qualitative data:

Please write, in your own words, your reactions to the overall effectiveness of Sandra Wilson as the main workshop presenter.

Evaluation is usually most effective if both quantitative and qualitative data are collected. In this way, each approach to data collection serves as a check and balance for the other. Therefore, when planning either formative or summative evaluation, it is usually best to plan to collect both quantitative and qualitative data.

Tip 132
When constructing the quantitative part of an evaluation instrument, use either discrete categories or a continuum to indicate respondents' reactions.

Two modes are typically used to collect quantitative data on an evaluation. Instruments and their rating scales may force respondents to pick discrete categories or they may allow respondents to indicate their responses on a continuum. Either way is effective in providing good data. For example, here is a rating scale that forces respondents to pick discrete categories:

> How do you rate the effectiveness of the social events in helping people to meet each other and to discuss ideas?
>
> _____ Very effective
> _____ Above average
> _____ Average
> _____ Below average
> _____ Poor

Using this scale, respondents are forced to choose a category to indicate their reactions.

Another effective quantitative data collection scale is the continuum. This is an example of the same question that respondents can rate on a continuum without being forced to choose a single discrete category.

> How do you rate the effectiveness of the social events in helping people to meet each other and to discuss ideas?
>
> 1   2   3   4   5   6   7   8   9   10
> ───
> Poor   Very
>   good

Neither of these types of rating scales is better than the other. Both are equally effective, depending on how you wish to report your data. The advantage of the first one is that it is easier to attach a label to the rating respondents make. The advantage of the continuum rating scale is that it offers greater flexibility to indicate responses without having a response attached to a particular discrete label.

Try using both of these types of quantitative rating scales on evaluations. A little experimenting will usually indicate which you prefer for data collection. Or if you are like many program planners, you may find that you like to use both types, depending on the needs of the evaluation.

Tip 133
Consider carefully the wording for the labels on the evaluation scale.

Labels for responses on all rating scales need to be chosen with great care. In the examples in the previous tips, note that the word *excellent* is never used. This is because many program planners have found that if they use the word *excellent* to indicate a response, almost no one ever marks this category. Research on this issue tends to suggest that the higher the educational level of the audience, the less likely they are to rate anything as excellent.

On the other hand, if rating scales are constructed so that the word *excellent* is omitted and labels like *very good* are used instead, people are more willing to mark that response.

This can be a very sensitive issue for people who must review evaluation results. If small numbers of people evaluate a program as excellent, this may or may not mean that people did not enjoy it as much as they could have. It is possible that members of the group have been enculturated to be overly critical and never rate anything as excellent. A comment on a recent program evaluation illustrates this point very well. One respondent wrote: "I really enjoyed this program. However, I did not rate it as excellent because I don't think many things in the world are really excellent. There is always room for improvement."

Therefore, when deciding on labels for evaluation rating scales, consider carefully what those labels should be and how those data will be used. Experiment with various labels until you find the ones that work best for your needs. Do not fall into what can be a potential trap by automatically using the label *poor* for one end of the rating scale and *excellent* for the label at the other end.

Tip 134
Consider carefully the wording when you ask respondents to suggest areas for improvement in future programs.

Many evaluations for programs have the following two standard questions:

1. What did you like best about this program?

2. What did you like least about this program?

The second question can be a trap that can have severe political implications, depending on how you choose to interpret the data and who is interpreting them. For example, a respondent may be very pleased with the contents of the entire program, but since you ask people to list what they like least, many respondents will oblige by writing something down. They may have liked everything in the program, but they may have liked some parts of the program better than other parts. However, most people will interpret the data resulting from this response to mean that people did not like, rather than liked least, the things listed.

To avoid this no-win trap, eliminate asking people what they liked least. What you really want from such a response is for people to indicate what changes they would suggest for future programs in order to make them even more effective. Therefore, try the following wording to achieve this:

1.   What did you find to be most helpful about this program?

2.   If we were to repeat this program, can you suggest any changes that would improve it?

This last question more accurately gets at what you really wanted to know — what changes should be made in future programs. In addition, it avoids the trap of people listing things they liked least when they may have been generally satisfied with everything but might have liked some things better than others.

Tip 135
Always conduct evaluations in relation to clearly established goals.

One of the mistakes frequently made in evaluation is the failure to evaluate in relation to clearly established goals. When this happens, evaluation often becomes a popularity contest geared to ascertaining how much participants were entertained by various presentations. To avoid this, clearly establish the goals of a program and advertise them in all brochures or catalogues. Then include a statement of the program's goals in the registration packets, and review these goals at the opening of the program as part of the general welcome and information review. The idea is to have people approach each program session with the same set of expectations rather than developing expectations that may or may not be congruent with what you are trying to achieve.

For example, recently a large philanthropic foundation sponsored a two-and-a-half-day conference entitled "Critical Community Health Issues: Improving the Quality of Life for the Twenty-First Century." The program planners established the following three goals for the conference:

• To provide a retrospective of the foundation's funded programs in community health care during the previous ten years
• To articulate the lessons learned through these funded projects about community health care
• In light of these lessons, to anticipate future directions for community health care

The program was a special invitational conference for 125 health care leaders, and the goals were communicated clearly in the letters of invitation. In addition, the goals were included in letters of acknowledgment and the registration packet, and were mentioned during the introductory and concluding sessions during each day of the conference.

The evaluation was then designed to ascertain how well participants felt the conference had met its clearly stated goals. Exhibit 26 shows the evaluation instrument that was used to collect these data. Note how both quantitative and qualitative data are used and how the evaluation begins by asking people to indicate how successful the program was in achieving its stated goals.

**Exhibit 26. Evaluation Instrument for
the Educative Museum Conference.**

We would appreciate it if you would take a few minutes to give us some feedback regarding this conference. Thanks so much. We appreciate your help.

This conference had three major goals. Would you please give us your indication of how successful we were in achieving these goals.

1. Goal 1: To provide a retrospective of the foundation's funded programs in community health care during the previous ten years.

    _____ Very good
    _____ Good
    _____ Average
    _____ Below average
    _____ Poor

2. Goal 2: To articulate the lessons learned through these funded projects about community health care.

    _____ Very good
    _____ Good
    _____ Average
    _____ Below average
    _____ Poor

3. Goal 3: In light of the lessons learned, to anticipate future directions for community health care.

    _____ Very good
    _____ Good
    _____ Average
    _____ Below average
    _____ Poor

4. How would you rate the social events, meals, and breaks in giving you a chance to interact with other conference participants?

    _____ Very good
    _____ Good
    _____ Average
    _____ Below average
    _____ Poor

**Exhibit 26. Evaluation Instrument
for the Educative Museum Conference, Cont'd.**

---

5. Please rate your overall reaction to the conference.

____ Very good
____ Good
____ Average
____ Below average
____ Poor

6. What did you find to be most valuable about this conference?

7. What one or two ideas did you pick up from this conference that you think will be useful in your job?

8. Additional remarks:

Tip 136
Evaluation instruments that can be filled out in five minutes or less will draw a greater response rate than longer forms.

Generally speaking, most program participants will not take the time to fill out long, involved evaluation instruments. After all, they are doing you a favor in responding at all. Therefore, in order to ensure the largest number of responses possible and thus increase the effectiveness of your overall evaluation, design the evaluation instrument so that it is short and can be filled out in less than five minutes. This will increase the response rate, and the higher response rates increase the validity of your evaluation.

Tip 137
Consider designing short, easy-to-fill-out evaluations for individual program sessions that are part of a larger program.

Large programs with many individual concurrent presentations or workshops present special problems for evaluation. If you wait until the end of the program to conduct an evaluation, the following things may happen:

- A number of people may have travel schedules that require them to leave early. Thus, you may not receive evaluations from a significant portion of your audience.
- If the program is large and has many concurrent sessions, the evaluation form will have to be long and cumbersome in order to list every concurrent session. Long evaluations turn people off and decrease your response rate.
- People may not remember the names of presenters, particularly if the program lasts several days. As a result, they will not fill out the form or they may not be able to match their responses to the names of program presenters.

In order to counteract these negative issues of waiting until the end to conduct an evaluation of a long program with a number of concurrent sessions, conduct short, easy-to-fill-out evaluations at the end of each individual session. Station someone at the exit to the room to collect the evaluations as people leave. This will usually yield close to a 100 percent response rate. Exhibit 27 shows how to design a short evaluation instrument designed to achieve an almost total response rate in an effortless way from the audience for an individual program session.

Exhibit 27. Short Evaluation Form for Use at the End of Individual Program Sessions Within a Conference.

Won't you take a few moments to provide valuable feedback to us that will be helpful in planning future programs? Just complete this form and turn it in to the person at the door.

Title of this session _____

Name of presenter _____

1. Your overall reaction to this session:

    _____ Poor_____ Below _____ Average_____ Above _____ Very
                        average   average   good

2. What did you find to be most helpful about this session?

3. Do you have any suggestions for improvement in this session?

4. Additional remarks:

Tip 138
Use a listening group to report findings at the end of the program.

Listening groups are useful for involving key opinion makers in the process of program evaluation. Typically a listening group might have five to eight people who would attend all the major program sessions and selectively attend concurrent sessions. The purpose of the listening group is to identify major concerns, learnings, themes, and issues that emerge during the course of the program. Then at the end they report their impressions, either to the entire group of participants or to the program planners.

Listening groups are particularly effective given the following conditions:

- When the program is large.
- When many issues are being presented, particularly if there may be controversy over ideas being presented.
- When key opinion makers are critical to the success of a program. By involving them as roving listeners and ambassadors throughout the program, they are able to use their expertise to identify many important issues for future consideration.
- When key opinion makers are not on the program because of time limitations. Thus, you are able to incorporate their expertise through the debriefing of a listening panel.

Such listening groups are particularly effective for identifying issues and ideas that should be explored in future programs. Under these circumstances they can often identify major themes that should be addressed in upcoming programs and even suggest presenters to address these issues.

Tip 139
Use focus groups to assist with evaluation.

A technique similar to a listening panel that is useful for evaluation is focus groups. Focus groups and listening panels differ in one major way. A listening panel is usually composed of key opinion makers who are preselected to act as your eyes and ears throughout the program. Because they are key opinion makers, they are not necessarily representative of the average person attending. Focus groups, on the other hand, are usually selected randomly and thus tend to more closely represent the opinions of the average participant. Focus groups tend to be most effective if they are not preselected but instead are selected either immediately after a program or during one of the concluding program sessions.

Tip 140
Conduct a content analysis of what the participants identify as the most useful ideas presented during a program.

This is a very useful way to gather qualitative data. Using this method, you ask participants to identify their major learnings or the major important ideas they have found to be most helpful during the course of the program. Typically this is done as part of an overall written questionnaire. For example, here are some questions to consider for such a questionnaire:

- List four ideas that you found to be most helpful and that you might consider implementing back home on the job.
- What were the three most significant learnings you experienced as a result of attending this program?
- If you were describing this program to friends over lunch, what would you tell them regarding what you found to be most valuable as a result of attending?

When this information has been collected, sort it into natural, logical categories. Major categories of themes will begin to emerge. This information can be very helpful as you assess the effectiveness of your program as well as changes you might like to make in future programs.

Tip 141
Employ the services of an on-site, professional evaluator to gather data.

This is a very useful method that is usually combined with written questionnaires. When this method is used, a professional evaluator is hired to attend the program. That person attends sessions, chats with participants about their satisfaction with the program, and prepares a report. When using this method, it is helpful to identify the program evaluator to the audience at the beginning so that people will realize why they are being asked questions. In addition, this enables people with specific recommendations to seek out the evaluator to be sure that their recommendations are heard.

A good place to find effective professional evaluators is through local colleges and universities. Often in colleges of education or in special instructional development centers, there will be a number of people who are specially trained in this type of evaluation. These people are usually either professors or advanced graduate students trained in comprehensive evaluation.

Tip 142
Analyze key variables that can affect evaluation results.

Evaluation is not a pure process. Rather, it is a complex activity that is affected by a number of important variables. Therefore, consider these major variables when designing and conducting the evaluation:

- Evaluation done at the end of a long, strenuous day can be affected adversely by people who may be suffering from information overload.
- If an individual presenter is controversial and tends to polarize the audience, people often will react either very positively or very negatively to the presentation, with very few reactions in the middle. This should be considered when analyzing the results.
- If a program has been highly structured during an entire day, followed by dinner and an after-dinner presentation, the after-dinner presentation will tend to be rated lower than if the same person made the same presentation at the beginning of the day. Tired people give lower evaluations.
- If people are forced to choose between too many concurrent sessions so that they feel they have not been able to hear other sessions in which they are intensely interested, they will have a tendency to give everything a lower evaluation than if they feel they have been able to attend the major sessions and events they wanted.

Tip 143
There is a relationship between the energy people put forth to learn during a program and their overall satisfaction with the program.

The effectiveness of a program and its presentations is not entirely dependent on the presenters. Evaluation is also affected by the goals of the program, whether these goals are clearly stated, the expectations of the participants, and the energy that participants invest in their own learning. Therefore, consider acknowledging this and asking people to rate how much energy they put into directing their overall learning. Exhibit 28 shows how to include this issue on an evaluation questionnaire.

Exhibit 28. Evaluation Form Asking Respondents to Rate the Amount of Energy They Contributed to the Program.

[This evaluation instrument was designed to be used with an executive development program that had thirty-five participants from the same organization. The participants met for three days, followed by a month off, another day of workshops, followed by another month off, followed by a fifth day of workshops. Reading assignments were given between meetings, and participants were asked to meet once a week for two hours in study teams to discuss the implications of the ideas in their reading for their jobs.]

This executive development program had the following major goals:

1. To help you analyze yourself in your leadership position for the purpose of deciding how you might become even more effective in your many leadership roles.
2. To help you develop some specific strategies to use to improve your leadership effectiveness.
3. To help you become aware of the importance of making conscious choices related to your leadership.

The effectiveness of any executive development program is directly related to the amount of work, effort, and energy you put into it. Please evaluate your perception of how hard you worked during the workshop sessions, the degree to which you completed the readings, and your attendance at and contribution to the weekly study team meetings.

Please check the statement below that most accurately describes your work at this program.

_____ 4. I completed all assignments and worked very hard in trying to find ways to improve my leadership.
_____ 3. I completed most things and worked hard during the workshops.
_____ 2. I put in an average amount of work.
_____ 1. I was below average in the amount of work I put in.

Please rate the effectiveness of the overall program in achieving its stated goals.

Goal: To help you analyze yourself in your leadership position for the purpose of deciding how you might become even more effective in your many leadership roles.

_____ 5. Very effective in meeting this goal
_____ 4. Effective
_____ 3. Somewhat effective

Exhibit 28. Evaluation Form Asking Respondents to Rate the Amount of Energy They Contributed to the Program, Cont'd.

_____ 2. Below average

_____ 1. Ineffective

Goal: To help you develop some specific strategies to use to improve your leadership effectiveness.

_____ 5. Very effective in meeting this goal

_____ 4. Effective

_____ 3. Somewhat effective

_____ 2. Below average

_____ 1. Ineffective

Goal: To help you become aware of the importance of making conscious choices related to your leadership.

_____ 5. Very effective in meeting this goal

_____ 4. Effective

_____ 3. Somewhat effective

_____ 2. Below average

_____ 1. Ineffective

My overall reaction to the entire executive development program was:

_____ 4. Very good

_____ 3. Good

_____ 2. Average

_____ 1. Below average

What did you find to be most helpful about the program?

Please list the three ideas you found to be most valuable for your present position.

1.

2.

3.

Additional comments:

Evaluations that ask participants to assess how hard they worked at directing their own learning tend to work best under the following conditions:

- When the program is of an executive development nature and consists of smaller numbers of participants
- When sessions have been designed to include homework, supplemental readings, and other activities to be completed outside the formal sessions
- When the program activities have been deliberately designed to actively engage participants through activities such as exercises, simulations, case studies, and study teams that are required to complete specific assignments

Tip 144
Do not try to evaluate everything.

There is a tendency in any evaluation to try to evaluate everything, but this is simply not possible. Keeping in mind that a goal of effective evaluation for conferences and workshops is to keep any evaluation instrument short so that it can be filled out in five minutes or less, consider omitting such evaluation questions as the following:

- How would you rate the coffee breaks? (There are other, more important items than this to evaluate.)
- How do you rate the meals? (You can usually determine this for yourself by eating the meals.)
- How would you rate the advertising for the program? (People generally cannot remember very well what the advertising was.)
- How do you rate the meeting facilities? (You can usually determine this yourself.)
- How do you rate your hotel room? (Again, you can usually determine this yourself.)

While it is useful to have data related to the above questions, if the evaluation is to be short, it is usually not possible to include such items. Therefore, consider carefully whether or not you can assess effectively the answers to any questions on the evaluation instrument by chatting informally with participants or by using your own judgment.

Tip 145
Plan evaluation data for component parts of a program, such as individual presentations by speakers, so that they relate to the overall program evaluation.

Exhibits 29 and 30 show how to design evaluations for the overall program so that they are compatible with evaluation data for individual sessions. These sample evaluations are for a thirty-day advanced executive development institute held at a large university. Exhibit 29 illustrates the short, easy-to-fill-out evaluation for the entire program. Exhibit 30 is the evaluation used for individual presentations. Note that the goal of each individual session is clearly spelled out, so that the evaluation of the session begins in relation to this clearly stated goal.

Exhibit 29. Evaluation Instrument
for the Advanced Executive Development Institute.

Overall Reaction to the Program

For the following questions, please indicate your ratings using the following scale:

> 5 = Very good
> 4 = Good
> 3 = Average
> 4 = Fair
> 1 = Poor
> 0 = Not applicable

_____ 1. The overall goal of this advanced executive development institute was to provide you with a thirty-day, residential learning experience away from your job so that you could study, analyze, and learn new ideas and strategies to help make you even more effective in your job. How well was this goal met?

_____ 2. How do you rate the level of efforts you applied to study during the institute?

_____ 3. How do you rate your attempts to seek clarification of ideas, particularly those you did not understand as well as you would like?

_____ 4. To what degree have you gained information, ideas, and/or methods to help you improve your management skills?

_____ 5. To what degree has your participation in study teams assisted your learning and understanding of the topic?

_____ 6. To what degree has your participation in study teams assisted your learning and understanding of group process?

7. Have there been concerns that have not been adequately covered or not addressed at all? If so, what are they?

Exhibit 30. Rating Form for Individual Presentations.

Presenter's Name: William Sampson

Topic: Designing Electronic Spreadsheets to Do Long-Range Budget Planning

Goal: The goal of this session was to demonstrate how you can design an electronic spreadsheet that will assist you in doing long-range budget planning and forecasting.

Please use the following scale to evaluate this session in questions 1 to 5 that follow:

> 5 = Very good
> 4 = Good
> 3 = Average
> 4 = Fair
> 1 = Poor
> 0 = Not applicable

How well did the session:

_____ 1. Achieve its goal, which is stated above?
_____ 2. Introduce you to new ideas?
_____ 3. Provide relevant information that you can adapt for use back home on the job?
_____ 4. Gear the instruction to your level of understanding and expertise?
_____ 5. Adequately provide opportunity for questions and discussion?
       6. Additional comments:

Source: Planning and Marketing Conferences and Workshops: Tips, Tools, and Techniques, by Robert G. Simerly. San Francisco: Jossey-Bass. Copyright ©1990. Permission granted to reproduce.

Tip 146
Use evaluation as a form of program improvement.

Program evaluation usually has two basic purposes: (1) to describe respondents' reactions to what took place and (2) to suggest ways to improve future programs. Therefore, after collecting, tabulating, and reporting evaluation results, carefully analyze the implications the evaluation has for future programming. In order to provide a structured way to achieve this, design and use an evaluation analysis sheet similar to the one in Exhibit 31. This becomes a helpful, structured way to focus your attention on major conclusions from the evaluation.

Exhibit 31. Program Evaluation Analysis Worksheet.

List the major trends, ideas, or issues that emerged as a result of the evaluation.

1.
2.
3.
4.

If you, as the program planner, could design the program again, knowing what you know now, what would you do differently?

1.
2.
3.
4.

If you could design the evaluation again, knowing what you know now, what would you do differently?

1.
2.
3.
4.

Additional comments:

Summary

This chapter has emphasized the need to do both formative and summative evaluation for conferences and workshops. In addition, the importance of collecting both quantitative and qualitative data has been highlighted. It is important to conduct all evaluations in relation to clearly established goals, and all the sample instruments in this chapter have been designed to achieve this. Suggestions have been given for how to word the labels on evaluation scales, with the suggestion that the term *excellent* be omitted from all labels. In addition to questionnaires, alternatives such as listening groups, focus groups, and using a professional evaluator have been suggested.

The goal of this chapter has been to stimulate thinking related to the process of evaluation. The sample evaluation instruments have all been designed to be short enough to be filled out in five minutes, and they combine qualitative and quantitative data collection. And most of all, they can easily be redesigned and adapted to meet the individual needs of almost all conferences and workshops.

Exhibit 32. Checklist for Designing Successful Evaluations.

This checklist is useful to review as an integral part of planning any evaluation process. It contains reminders related to the major suggestions offered in this chapter.

_____ 1. Have you clearly distinguished between formative and summative evaluation?

_____ 2. Have you considered personal or focus group interviews as a way to collect formative evaluation data?

_____ 3. If you use interviews for formative evaluation, have you developed a written, structured interview format for collecting data?

_____ 4. Have you provided for collecting both quantitative and qualitative data on evaluation instruments if it is appropriate to do so?

_____ 5. Have you developed logical reasons for using either discrete categories or a continuum to indicate respondents' reactions?

_____ 6. Have you carefully developed the appropriate wording for all evaluation scales?

_____ 7. Have you avoided asking what people liked least about a program?

_____ 8. Have you designed all summative evaluations around clearly established goals?

_____ 9. Can all instruments be filled out in five minutes or less?

_____ 10. Have you considered developing short, easy-to-fill-out evaluations for individual program sessions that are part of a larger program?

_____ 11. Is a listening group appropriate for your evaluation process?

_____ 12. Are focus groups appropriate for your evaluation?

_____ 13. Have you planned for a content analysis of major themes that emerge from an analysis of qualitative data?

_____ 14. Have you considered employing an on-site evaluator?

_____ 15. If it is appropriate to do so, have you asked people to rate how much energy they devoted to directing their own learning?

_____ 16. Has evaluation of any individual presentation been related to clearly stated goals?

Source: Planning and Marketing Conferences and Workshops: Tips, Tools, and Techniques, by Robert G. Simerly. San Francisco: Jossey-Bass. Copyright ©1990. Permission granted to reproduce.

7

Staying on
the Cutting Edge:

Twenty-Six Tips for
Conducting Ongoing
Market Research and Analysis

In order to plan for the long-term growth of conferences and workshops, it is important to engage in a comprehensive research and analysis of your market, your programs, and your services. To achieve this, it is important to allocate the following three resources to this activity: time, human resources, and money. While it is difficult to suggest a percentage of income that should be allocated to this research because all organizations and their needs vary so widely, if you are spending less than 5 percent of your total income on market research, you probably should consider increasing this amount. Naturally, some organizations will need to spend more than this to achieve their marketing goals.

Conducting ongoing research is the key to continued program growth and development. It will keep you and your organization on the cutting edge of new developments in programs, products, and services. And most of all, it will provide reliable data for establishing an agenda for change, setting new directions for the future, and thus providing a process for constant organizational renewal.

The basic premise of this chapter is that you do not need to hire outside consultants to do research for you. There is a wide variety of research that you can conduct yourself. This chapter provides many practical, easy-to-implement tips for conducting effective, action-oriented research designed to improve the marketing of your conferences and workshops.

Tip 147
Plan for developing a comprehensive research base related to marketing activities.

Much has been written about market research and, as a result, marketing has developed into an academic discipline with specialized language, concepts, techniques, and guidelines for effective practice. Conducting effective market research involves becoming a behavioral scientist who constantly finds new and effective ways to study the behavior of people in relation to programs, products, and services. Framing this issue within a context of becoming a behavioral scientist means that successful market researchers tend to avoid pat, prescriptive solutions to marketing problems. Instead, they concentrate on developing an ongoing, action-oriented research base useful in helping them design better strategies appropriate for the special needs of their organization.

Tip 148
Build a carefully thought-out organizational data base of reliable information.

The key to long-term success in conducting research is building a reliable data base related to your market, programs, and services. For example, here are some of the issues for which it is important to build a long-term data base:

- What is the average registration rate for direct-mail brochures per 1,000 items mailed?
- What variables can be manipulated to increase or decrease this response rate?
- What reliable and systematic processes can be developed to collect data on how people perceive the quality of your programs and services?
- What is the appropriate marketing mix among direct mail, newspaper and magazine advertising, public relations, and personal sales?
- How can you institute processes that will be effective in developing new program ideas directly related to the needs of the wide variety of your customers?
- How do you establish reliable feedback channels to find out whether your copy and graphic design convey the image and tone you have determined to be appropriate for your organization?
- Do you have reliable tracking systems so that mailing lists composed of past participants can easily be put together in appropriate ways for advertising new programs?
- How do you get feedback on the effectiveness of your staff in handling telephone requests for information and registrations?
- How do you determine your effectiveness in marketing? For example, have you developed agreed-on measures of effectiveness or do you tend

to assume that no matter how effective your marketing is, it is not successful enough? This latter approach can have a severe negative effect on staff morale. The former can help establish a positive working environment that will contribute to increasing morale.

- What portion of your budget is allocated for direct and indirect marketing costs? Often this is broken down into a portion for each individual program budget as well as a portion of the overall organizational budget for general marketing activities.
- Does this marketing budget need to be increased or decreased?
- How do you compare in marketing effectiveness with other organizations that are similar to you? Do you spend more or less on marketing? Are you more effective or less effective in your marketing efforts? Is the return on marketing investment greater or less than that of the competition?
- What kind of training and development activities have you established to help keep all staff on the cutting edge of excellent practice in marketing?
- How do you reward staff for excellence in marketing effectiveness?

You can solve organizational problems using your research data and behavioral science action-oriented research methods. Developing this conceptual base of behavioral science research techniques, learning how to interpret research data and make reliable inferences from them, and building a research base appropriate to the special needs of your programs will have important, long-term payoffs.

Tip 149
Conduct a market audit.

A first step in developing research related to conferences and workshops is to conduct a market audit. This can be as elaborate or as simple as you desire to make it. You can use outside consultants or do it yourself. The following tips demonstrate easy ways to do this yourself. Figure 2 illustrates a useful way to plan for the component parts of a market audit.

In quadrant 1 list all of your marketing activities that are effective and working well for your programs. Identifying these items will serve as an important reminder to maintain these effective activities. In quadrant 2 list all of the marketing activities that need improvement but are amenable to change if someone can come up with a better way of doing things. In quadrant 3 list all of the marketing functions that are working well and thus would be difficult to change if anyone attempted to do so. In quadrant 4 list all of the marketing functions that need improvement but will be difficult to change. Then in quadrant 5 list all future directions or strategies you should consider.

This short, easy-to-use model can be used by one person or by an entire staff. When using it with more than one person, get your staff together,

Figure 2. Market Audit Model.

	Effective	Needs improvement	
Easy to change	Quadrant 1	Quadrant 2	Describes current conditions
Hard to change	Quadrant 3	Quadrant 4	
	Quadrant 5 Future directions		List activities for the future

explain the component parts of the model, and ask people to list things in the appropriate quadrants. This always elicits lively discussion and is a very energizing process. Tapping the suggestions of an entire staff usually yields a wealth of new ideas on how to enhance marketing activities. Through further discussion and analysis you can develop priorities for activities and strategies that need to be tackled first.

Tip 150
Decide in advance the goals you want to achieve with a market audit.

Like any organizational audit, it is important to establish in advance your goals for conducting an audit. Some of these goals might be:

- To create an agenda for changing some of your marketing activities
- To identify strategies that are working well so you can take steps to ensure that you maintain these strategies

- To help educate staff regarding the importance of the marketing function by involving them in the critique and analysis of your total marketing efforts
- To identify market niches that are not being served so that you can develop new programs in these areas
- To find out what your competition does well or poorly

By having clearly in mind the goals you want to achieve with an audit, it is easy to build into the process ways to achieve them. Also, when you involve staff in the audit process, it helps speed the process along if they clearly understand what goals you are trying to achieve. Then they can frame their suggestions within the context of attaining these goals.

Tip 151
Diligently research your competition.

Essential to successful marketing is researching your competition. The four most common areas where you need accurate data regarding your competition are related to (1) the content of their programs, (2) their client service orientation when people call or write for more information or want to register, (3) their total registration service orientation, and (4) how they handle people on site during their programs. Develop effective ways to collect reliable data in each of these areas. For example, you should:

1. Get on the mailing list of your competition. If necessary, give your home mailing address so as not to tip off the competition if you have reason to believe that they will not welcome a competitor's name and address on their list. Or get a friend to get on the mailing list and give you all the mail received.
2. Call and represent yourself as a person who wants more information about some of their programs. Analyze how their staff deals with your concerns to find out if it is effective or ineffective.
3. Register for some of their programs. In this way you can analyze how they handle you as a customer from the time you register until you show up on site.
4. Attend some of their programs. Observe how they handle people. Judge the quality of the program, the content, and the presenters. Get a feel for the general ambience they create. Do you feel welcomed or do they keep you at a distance? Do they give you personal service or treat you like a number in the crowd?

It is through this ongoing, thorough analysis of your competition that you will be able to decide how you can position your organization and its programs in special marketing niches that are underserved by the competition. You can learn a lot just by observing and analyzing the competition. Not only can you learn what to do effectively, but you can also often learn what not to do.

Tip 152
Research the overall, instant image people have of your organization and its programs.

An easy way to do this is to conduct personal interviews either face-to-face or over the phone. These can be short and to the point since you are looking for their responses that represent their gut-level, instant image they carry around regarding your organization and its programs. Select a random sample of your target audience. Such an interview can be as simple as asking a few questions and recording, clarifying, and analyzing the responses. Exhibit 33 shows a sample interview sheet for guiding your questions and recording responses. Be sure to instruct interviewers to record the person's responses accurately. It is the exact words of the responders that will yield rich data. Do not allow these data to be filtered and possibly changed by the interviewer.

**Exhibit 33. Interview Script to Determine
Customer's Image of Your Organization and Its Programs.**

"Hello, my name is _____. I am conducting research on what people think of [insert the name of your organization]. I have several short questions that I would like to ask you regarding how you see us. May I have three or four minutes of your time?" [When permission to proceed has been obtained, continue.]

"When I ask you the question, it will be most helpful if you can answer quickly with the first words you think of."

1. "When you think of [insert the name of your organization], please say the words that immediately come to your mind." [Note: They may not have heard of you. If not, thank them, tell them some important facts about your organization and its programs, and terminate the interview.]

2. "If you were describing [insert the name of your organization] and its programs to a friend privately over lunch, how would you describe us?"

3. "What things do you particularly like about our organization and its programs?"

4. "What advice can you give us about what we need to change?"

5. "Do you have any other responses that could assist us as we study our image?"

"Thanks for your time. We really appreciate it. The information you have given us will be extremely helpful in assisting us to serve you and the community more effectively with our conferences, institutes, workshops, and meetings."

Source: Planning and Marketing Conferences and Workshops: Tips, Tools, and Techniques, by Robert G. Simerly. San Francisco: Jossey-Bass. Copyright ©1990. Permission granted to reproduce.

Tip 153
Research what customers perceive to be the special benefits they received as a result of attending your programs.

All programs have special benefits people feel they obtain as a result of attending. In fact, communicating clearly these special benefits is an important motivator in getting people to register. You know what you believe to be special benefits people receive from your programs. In addition, it is important to determine what your customers perceive to be your special benefits. These may not always be the same.

Data regarding this can be obtained through either interviewing or written surveys. Exhibit 34 shows how to collect these data through interviews, and Exhibit 35 illustrates how to use a written survey for collecting these data. Both of these ways are short and easy to use. Note that both techniques make use of an open-ended survey approach. This is because you want to know in the customers' own words what they think to be your special program benefits. You can then use these exact words in your brochure copy. Stating special benefits in the exact words of your past participants can constitute your most powerful, motivating advertising copy.

**Exhibit 34. Interview Script for
Determining Customer Perceptions of Special
Benefits of Your Organization and Its Programs.**

"Hello. My name is _____, and I am calling for [insert the name of your organization]. We are calling people who have attended our programs in the past to determine what they feel are special benefits they have received as a result of attending. Our records indicate that you attended [insert the name of the program] on [insert date]. Is that correct?"

_____ Yes   _____ No

[If no, correct the information.]

"I would appreciate it if you could give me several minutes of your time to respond to five short questions." [Wait to secure an okay.]

1. "As you think back about the program, what do you feel are special benefits you received as a result of attending?"

2. "If you were describing the program to a friend, what would you describe as the special benefits your friend could obtain as a result of attending a similar program?"

3. "How has the program helped you to do a better job at work [or at home if the content was related to personal rather than organizational issues]?"

4. "We are writing brochure copy for a similar program. Can you suggest any special benefits that we should be sure to include?"

5. "Do you have any additional remarks about the special benefits you received as a result of attending?"

"Thanks so much for your time. We certainly appreciate it. Your responses will help us do a better job of serving other customers such as you."

Source: Planning and Marketing Conferences and Workshops: Tips, Tools, and Techniques, by Robert G. Simerly. San Francisco: Jossey-Bass. Copyright ©1990. Permission granted to reproduce.

Exhibit 35. Written Survey for Determining What Customers Perceive to Be the Major Benefits from Attending Your Program.

We need your help. We are trying to find the most effective way possible to communicate to the public the benefits people have received from attending our programs.

Won't you take a few minutes to respond to this short survey? Your responses are important and will enable us to do a better job serving people like you.

Thanks.

1. As a result of attending this program, can you identify four major benefits you have received?
   1.
   2.
   3.
   4.

2. If you were to describe to a friend several other benefits you have received, what would they be?
   1.
   2.
   3.
   4.
   5.

Overall, how would you rate the benefits you have received as a result of attending this program? (Please circle the number to indicate response.)

5	4	3	2	1
Very effective	Effective	Average	Not very effective	Ineffective

Source: Planning and Marketing Conferences and Workshops: Tips, Tools, and Techniques, by Robert G. Simerly. San Francisco: Jossey-Bass. Copyright ©1990. Permission granted to reproduce.

In order to get the best possible responses from the written survey in Exhibit 35, allow time toward the end of a program for it to be handed out, completed, and collected. If you explain to your audience very clearly that you are doing action-oriented research designed to help serve people like them more effectively, most people will gladly assist you. The information they provide can prove to be invaluable as you research what people perceive to be the special benefits of your program.

Tip 154
Find out why people do *not* register for your programs.

It is relatively easy to find out why people register for your programs— just ask them and they will usually tell you. However, it is often difficult to engage in research designed to find out why people do not attend your programs. Having this information can be invaluable as you plan the future growth and operation of your organization. Here are two approaches to this very difficult and sometimes illusive issue:

• Keep a list of people who cancel their registrations before attending. Call them to ask why they canceled. For example, you may find that all of them had logical reasons for canceling, such as a conflict in schedule. However, you may also find that people canceled for other reasons. It is these other reasons that you want to know about and that can provide valuable research for helping you in planning future programs.

• After you have mailed out your direct-mail brochure, conduct a telephone survey in an effort to try to determine why people did not register. Exhibit 36 illustrates a sample script that can be used.

Exhibit 36. Script for Telephone Survey to Determine Why People Did Not Register for Your Program.

"Hello, my name is _____ and I am with [insert the name of your organization]. Recently we mailed you a brochure describing [insert the title of your program] to take place on [insert date] at [insert location]. Do you remember seeing such a brochure come across your desk?"

_____ Yes   _____ No

[If no, probe to find out if the mail has been sorted by a secretary and may not have reached the person. Or perhaps there are other reasons. For example, maybe the reason they don't remember the brochure is that it wasn't bold enough to attract their attention. Whether the response is yes or no, at this point prompt the person with some details about the content of the program.]

"We are conducting research to try to determine why people chose not to register for this program in an effort to serve our clients in your profession better. Could you share with me the reasons why you did not consider registering for this program?"

[If the person cannot offer concrete reasons, you might still collect valuable information. Try quoting the registration fee and asking for reactions. Try gaining reactions about the time, date, and location. Try to ascertain whether or not the title and content appealed to them. Ask whether or not their employer pays for attendance at such programs. The idea here is that if people cannot remember receiving your brochure, this, alone, says that you may have to redesign it so that it is more vivid and eye-catching. Even though they may throw it away, you want them to have remembered it and think positively about your organization's programs.]

Source: Planning and Marketing Conferences and Workshops: Tips, Tools, and Techniques, by Robert G. Simerly. San Francisco: Jossey-Bass. Copyright ©1990. Permission granted to reproduce.

Tip 155
Consider the life cycle of programs.

Action-oriented research that gives accurate descriptions of how people respond to your programs is the best way to develop new programs as well as to modify existing programs. And remember, all programs have a definite life cycle. They rarely can exist from year to year without some modification. These are some of the steps in the product life cycle of any program:

- *Beginning.* You have a terrific idea for a new program and it is successful. You attract the required number of people to break even financially.
- *Building an audience.* Because of your previous success, you repeat the program. People keep signing up. Basically you do not tamper with the program content or advertising because you are successful and you do not want to spoil a good thing.
- *Peak performance.* This represents the high point of your success. From this point, registrations for the program begin to decline.
- *Losing your audience.* You now begin to modify the content, title, and advertising for the program. Some things work and some things do not. Registrations continue to decline slowly. Eventually you begin losing money.
- *Termination.* Your losses are now such that you terminate the program. A certain sadness prevails. You often have that gnawing feeling that if you had done things differently, you might have salvaged the program for a little longer.

This is the classical life cycle for almost all goods, products, and services that are marketed. Conferences and workshops are no exception. Nothing lasts forever. The important thing is to analyze your program and its accompanying marketing plan at each phase of the cycle, realizing that your program will probably move through this predictable cycle. If you treat the movement of programs through this life cycle as natural, it quickly becomes clear that you have two main jobs: (1) to constantly create new programs that will enter at the beginning of the marketing cycle and (2) to move each program through its logical progression of the predictable life cycle. If you conceptualize things this way and if you do your best to make the necessary adjustments at each phase of the marketing cycle, then it will not be so painful when you eventually have to make the decision to terminate. This is because you will always have fresh, innovative ideas to convert to new programs that will begin the program life cycle all over again.

Tip 156
Clearly identify the type of research you need to conduct.

There are four basic types of research that planners of conferences and workshops need to do — (1) exploratory, (2) descriptive, (3) predictive, and (4) feedback research. Each type has a different purpose, and different techniques tend to be associated with each type. Here are examples of how each of these types is used:

1. *Exploratory research.* This is the tentative research that begins to ferret out new program ideas and ways to test the market for interest in these new programs. It starts formulating ideas that can turn into proposals for development of new conferences and workshops.

This research is characterized by its tentativeness, elusiveness, difficulty, frustration, and sometimes an obtuse and disorganized approach. The reason for this is often you do not really know what you are looking for; therefore, it is difficult to clearly formulate ways to research the issues involved. Another way of saying this is that exploratory research leads to a lot of dead ends.

2. *Descriptive research.* This type generally is concrete. The researcher is observing and describing what exists. For example, you might conduct descriptive research by analyzing a direct-mail brochure to determine its strengths and weaknesses according to what you know generally works well for direct-mail brochures.

Descriptive research is characterized by its concreteness, the quickness and ease with which data can usually be collected, and the examples that can be used to illustrate the conclusions you reach as a result of analyzing data.

3. *Predictive research.* This type has a primary goal of researching ways to predict how people will react in the future. For example, you can work with an advisory group of fifteen personnel managers in planning a workshop designed for supervisors. The thrust of the workshop is to help supervisors become more aware of legal issues related to working with employees in order to keep the organization out of legal difficulties. You can conduct predictive research with this group by asking such questions as the following:

- How much would you be willing to pay for such a program?
- What are the five most common mistakes supervisors in your organization make in regard to legal issues?
- What benefits do you think your employees could obtain from attending such a workshop?
- When should this workshop be held? Days? Month? Time of day?
- How long should the workshop be in order to cover the topic adequately and minimize the time people would have to be away from work?

Predictive research is characterized by its tentativeness and the difficulty in guaranteeing results. Even the most carefully conducted predictive research cannot guarantee that enough people will actually register for a program. However, the more predictive research you do, the more accurate and reliable your predictions tend to become. This is because, like with all types of research, you make mistakes when actually doing the research and you learn from these mistakes.

4. *Feedback research.* This type has a single important goal. It is to collect data that can be fed back to the organization with the expressed pur-

pose of confirming that everything is okay or that something needs to be changed. For example, a typical form of feedback research occurs in a program evaluation when you ask the question "If you were planning a program similar to this one in the future, what could you suggest to make it even more effective?"

The characteristic of feedback research is that sometimes it is conducted but the results are not effectively converted to change strategies by the sponsoring organization. Feedback research can be very threatening, depending on the data uncovered. Therefore, usually staff, advisory boards, planning committees, or program planners have to be forewarned about the findings of feedback research—particularly if sensitive, negative issues emerge as a result of the data collection.

These four forms of research have very different goals, techniques, and dynamics behind them. Because of this, it is important to distinguish clearly what type of research needs to be done before undertaking it. In this way it is possible to clearly relate the type of research to your overall research goals to see if there is congruity between these two issues. Doing this will help to maximize the success of obtaining reliable data, analyzing it effectively, and presenting your findings in a form that will attract the attention of the people it was designed to help.

Tip 157
Use both quantitative and qualitative research methods for collecting data.

Quantitative research methods yield data that can easily be coded, tabulated, and reported. If it has numbers, it is quantitative. For example, a survey that asks people to rate things according to a numerical scale such as the one below yields quantitative data.

How would you rate the overall effectiveness of this program?

5	4	3	2	1
Very effective	Effective	Average	Not very effective	Ineffective

Qualitative research methods yield data that are not so easy to code, tabulate, or report. They usually consist of people's verbal reactions to things. For example, if a person says the following on an evaluation, it is qualitative data: "This is the best program on income tax preparation I have ever attended in my twenty-five years as a professional tax preparer!"

Both quantitative and qualitative data are reliable. Neither is better than the other. The issue of which to use should always be related to the goals of the research, what kind of research you are doing, how the data will be reported, and what action steps will be expected to be implemented as a result of the data. Indeed, many people who conduct research find that a combination of quantitative and qualitative data works best for them on most research projects.

Tip 158
Collect and analyze demographic data.

Demographic data refers to those items that are relatively easy to quantify and are basically nondisputable data about people in the marketplace. This typically includes such things as the number of people who are registered to vote in a community, occupational titles, the average number of children residing in households, age, race, income, and geographic area. If you are a program planner, you are probably already collecting many important demographic data about your program attendees. For example, you will probably collect data that include at least city, state, zip code, and occupational title. Maintaining an internal, computerized data system with codes for important demographic data for your current and past program registrants is essential to improving the research capability in your organization. If you have these data, you can use them in a variety of ways to assist you in your total marketing efforts. For example, you can:

- Generate mailing labels by zip code
- Generate labels by title of program
- Generate labels by interest area — such as all people who have taken an executive development program on strategic planning
- Generate labels for people who have phoned in to inquire about programs
- Generate labels for all people who registered for programs but canceled before attending

Demographic data are the most commonly collected data for registrants of conferences and workshops because they are the easiest to collect.

Tip 159
Collect and analyze behavioristic data.

Behavioristic data describe the way people behave. For example, what products do they buy? What types of cultural events do they attend? To what organizations do they donate money? How often do they take vacations and where do they go?

One of the most important types of behavioristic data that meeting planners can collect is data related to when registrations for a program come in. Carefully tracking this type of data provides excellent clues regarding how far in advance of a program advertising brochures should be mailed.

Tip 160
Collect and analyze psychographic data in order to improve the sophistication of your research.

Psychographic data are gaining in popularity and represent new ways to study audiences (Mitchell, 1983). Psychographic data describe life-style orientation. They describe the values people have, the life-styles they lead, and how this influences their spending patterns. Among the important issues in psychographic research data are the following: What expectations do people have for themselves and their children? How do people in different occupations react to various forms of media advertising? Who are the early adopters of change and new ideas?

Providers of conferences and workshops are now beginning to incorporate psychographic data into their market research. They are yielding some very interesting results.

Mitchell (1983) describes these life-style orientations through what he calls the VALS (values, attitudes, life-styles) topology. The VALS topology has important implications for program planners researching their markets. While it is not possible here to go into detailed analysis of the many detailed aspects of the VALS topology that helped legitimate psychographic data as an important data source for market researchers, the Mitchell book *The Nine American Lifestyles* provides a comprehensive overview of psychographic research.

Tip 161
Pilot-test titles for programs before actually printing direct-mail brochures.

Accurate, attention-grabbing titles can often make the difference between programs that are perceived as exciting and worthwhile and programs that sound mediocre. For example, if the target group to receive a direct-mail brochure for a one-day workshop is supervisory personnel in business, industry, social service agencies, education, and government, which program title would be more effective in attracting them — "Basic Introduction to Dealing with Difficult Customers" or "How to Cope with Upset Citizens: Turning Complainers into Allies for Your Organization"?

Or consider this example for a two-day conference for CPAs and others who deal with filling out income tax forms. Which title would most likely attract attention and make this target group consider the program to be valuable — "IRS Update for CPAs" or "How to Save Your Clients Every Dollar Possible on Their Taxes: The Latest Update on IRS Regulations for the New Tax Season"?

Creating accurate, motivating, and attention-getting titles is essential to direct-mail advertising success. In order to be as effective as possible, consider undertaking the following research:

• You want to write the title from the recipient's point of view. This means that the title must be motivating enough to make the target recipients feel the program deals with expert information, provides the latest update on the topic, and is practical and deals with their actual problems. For example, in the last example the title is highly motivating. CPAs who can save their clients money become known for this fact and this, in turn, creates excellent word-of-mouth advertising about their competence. This leads to new business. Thus, even though the title is rather long, its length is overcome by the fact that the title is practical, attention-getting, and highly motivating.

How do you achieve this? Write out a comprehensive outline of the entire content for a program. Jot down ten possible program titles. Get together several CPAs who are part of the target group to whom you will be mailing your brochures and run the titles by them. They will quickly tell you which are winners and which are losers. What you will probably find is that none of your ten actually turns out to be the one you use. Instead, as a result of your conversation you will probably be better able to see the world from their point of view and develop a title that is even better and more motivating than any of the ten you thought up.

• Effective program titles should have a sense of practical immediacy. Before they register for a program, adult learners want an answer to the question "Can I learn practical things that I can start using tomorrow?" Research can help determine exactly what people want to learn and under what conditions.

• Titles should indicate, whenever possible, how the program will benefit the attendee. In the previous example, learning ways to help clients save money is a highly motivating feature to register for the program. The benefit to attendees is the appreciation they will receive from their clients when they actually help them save money. This, in turn, should bring them more business as word is spread about their expertise.

• Action verbs are almost always more appropriate than passive verbs. Create copy describing the content using action verbs and ask representatives of your target audience to give their reactions to it.

• Titles should communicate a sense of the dynamic quality of the program. Again, ask representatives of your target audience what needs to be included in order for them to feel that the program is dynamic and will meet their immediate, practical needs.

This is action-oriented research at its best. Use it, hone your skills in conducting it, and integrate your findings in order to create the best possible dynamic, motivating program titles.

Tip 162
Be aware that surveys of possible program ideas have an inherent danger built into them.

People respond to surveys of interest in program topics for many reasons. They may want to please the surveyor, or perhaps they just want to cooperate. Often they will express interest in many ideas, but that does not necessarily mean they will register for programs based on these ideas.

Sometimes program planners send out well-designed surveys and have them returned indicating a high degree of interest in many of the proposed topic areas for new programs. Do not fall into the trap of believing that interest in a topic will necessarily result in registrations. Research in this area cannot always be that predictive. In order for people to actually register, the program must appeal to needs other than just expressed interest. For example, the registration fee needs to be affordable. The time, place, and dates need to be convenient. People must feel they will get their needs met as a result of attending. Therefore, an interest survey should be expanded to seek additional information. Exhibit 37 illustrates what a short interest survey can look like when it seeks to obtain this additional information.

Exhibit 37. Program Interest Survey.

We need your help. We are considering offering several new programs as part of our very successful series of one-day workshops. Won't you take a few minutes to fill out this survey and return it to us in the stamped, self-addressed envelope?

Please respond to the following:

1. To what extent would you be interested in attending a one-day workshop on the use of electronic spreadsheets for small business applications? (Please circle your choice.)

4	3	2	1
Very interested	Interested	Somewhat interested	Not interested

2. Would you actually attend such a workshop?

5	4	3	2	1
Definitely	Probably	Maybe	Not sure	No

3. If so, how much would you be willing to pay for a one-day workshop on electronic spreadsheets? _____

4. What are the best days for you to attend? (Check all that apply.)

_____ Monday   _____ Thursday   _____ Sunday
_____ Tuesday   _____ Friday
_____ Wednesday   _____ Saturday

5. What months are most convenient for you?

---

6. Additional comments:

Thanks for responding. We appreciate your help in assisting us to find ways to serve you better.

Tip 163
Use focus groups to collect valuable information.

Focus groups are groups of people you ask to meet together and chat about their reactions to your organization and its programs. They work best when done in an informal setting, such as around a conference table, where the tone and discussion are relaxed and conducive to thoughtful conversation. Generally focus groups consist of from five to ten people.

Conducting this type of research can provide valuable insights into how others view your programs as well as your organization as a whole. As the interviewer, you usually have a series of questions for which you would like to have answers. In addition, you need to allow for other reactions that may emerge as the group engages in conversation.

The advantages of focus groups are that (1) they are easy to assemble and use; (2) they are inexpensive because people generally do not receive money for participating, though you may offer them a free program registration of their choice; (3) they offer a rich source of data; and (4) it is easy to pursue additional topics important to your market research as the focus group chats.

The major disadvantages are that sometimes people want to please the interviewer so they do not necessarily give their most truthful responses. Also, there is the subjectivity of the interviewer to consider. In addition, because the sample is so small it may be difficult to generalize to the broader population.

Most market researchers, however, feel that the advantages of focus groups far outweigh the disadvantages. Focus groups can open up new avenues of inquiry through the issues they raise. And it is through these new avenues of inquiry that you will be able to develop strategies for conducting additional research—research that is important but that you might not have thought of before.

Tip 164
Conduct personal interviews.

These may be done either face-to-face or over the phone. The advantages and disadvantages of the focus group also apply to interview situations. However, telephone interviewing is an especially effective, inexpensive, and easy way to conduct research. In addition, another advantage is that telephone interviews can help build positive public relations. Most people are willing to chat if they feel they can help you in some way. Therefore, the key to conducting effective telephone interviews is to have the interviewer explain at the beginning what organization he or she represents and how responding will assist that organization to do a better job at serving people like the person called.

Tip 165
Find out who pays the program fees for your registrants.

Conducting this type of research is crucial to pricing your programs correctly. For example, if an organization sending people is paying the registration fee plus travel, hotel, meals, and other expenses, often the specific dollar amount of the fee (within reason) is not the critical variable that will cause people to attend. Rather, the critical variable is often related to whether or not the program appears to be of sufficient quality that the organization feels that sending a person will have sufficient payoffs to justify the expense.

The following are easy ways to find out who pays the fee:

- Use focus groups representing the target group of potential attendees. They can usually provide reliable information on this.
- Ask for this information on the registration form of a repeating program. For example, you could put the following on the form:

What percentage of your registration fee is paid by you personally? _____ By your employer? _____

What percentage of your travel is paid by you personally? _____ By your employer? _____

What percentage of your meals and miscellaneous expenses is paid by you personally? _____ By your employer? _____

Who pays the registration fee is usually the most critical piece of data you need in order to decide the maximum amount you can charge. Individuals who pay their own registration and other expenses usually are reluctant to pay as high a fee as an organization sponsoring a registrant.

Tip 166
Do split-tests of brochures versus letters.

Sometimes elaborately designed brochures are not the best way to attract registrants. Do a split-test where you use identical copy. For half of your test mail a bold, eye-catching, professionally designed brochure. For the other half of your list, mail the identical copy in a different format — typed in letter or report format and enclosed in an envelope with a cover letter.

Many program planners report that this typed letter or report format will often outdraw more expensive brochures. This is especially true if your target audience consists of busy professionals who get many direct-mail brochures across their desks every day. Usually the critical variable is that your advertising must (1) look very different from routine junk mail and (2) look different from that of your competition.

Tip 167
Test a wide variety of other direct-mail strategies.

There are many other direct-mail strategies that you should test. For example, consider the following:

- Test to find out if using a window envelope rather than a plain envelope produces more registrants.
- Test to find out if putting a brochure in an envelope versus mailing it unfolded without an envelope works best.
- Test to see if using a postage stamp rather than postage from a printed indicia on a postage meter draws best.
- Try putting an eye-catching message on an envelope to see if this draws better than advertising enclosed in a plain envelope with just your return address.

The list of possibilities here is almost endless. Test. Test. Test. And then test some more. Doing this type of action-oriented research is the only way to determine which direct-mail strategies work best for you.

Tip 168
Test to find out if the same brochure mailed a second time to the same person but spaced several weeks apart increases registrations significantly enough to justify the expense.

Many program planners report that this double-mailing technique increases registrations from 15 to 25 percent. For example, assume that the first direct-mail brochure is received by a potential participant ten weeks before a program. Plan the second mailing of the same brochure to arrive four to six weeks before the program. This accomplishes the following:

- It reminds people that they have a second chance to register if they have not yet done so.
- It creates another opportunity to market the image of your organization and its programs.
- It creates a second opportunity for recipients to pass along the brochure to an interested colleague.

In order to analyze the results of this double-mailing test, code all lists differently for each of the two mailings. These codes will enable you to track the results of the double mailing afterwards to see how much the second one increased your registrations. Armed with these data, you can then decide how cost-effective this was and make plans to either (1) continue such tests to collect more data, (2) adopt the double-mailing technique for programs when appropriate, or (3) discontinue it because responses to the second mailing may not have achieved your goal of increasing registrations by a significant enough percentage to offset the expense involved.

Tip 169
Keep extensive files illustrating examples of good and bad marketing ideas.

You can conduct a great deal of good research on your competition by reviewing these files. In addition, they will provide useful examples to show to your graphic designer and help explain what works and does not work in direct-mail as well as newspaper and magazine advertising. These files are also useful for new staff members to review to provide an overview of the wide variety of possibilities for program ideas, direct-mail brochures, newspaper and magazine ads, and news releases.

Separate the files into three categories and label them *winners, losers,* and *acceptable but average.* It will soon become apparent whom you want to emulate with your marketing strategies. You can then take ideas from the file of winners and modify them to meet the needs of your own programs.

Tip 170
Research response times for how soon people register after receiving your advertising.

This is a particularly critical area. Develop a way to track the pattern of response time. For example, one organization tracked registration response time for a brochure that was mailed out ten weeks before a program. This is what they found:

- Within a week after receiving a brochure 9 percent of their registrants responded.
- In the second week 18 percent responded.
- In the third week 47 percent responded.
- In the fourth week 10 percent responded.
- In the fifth week 11 percent responded.
- In the sixth week 2 percent responded.
- Between the seventh and tenth weeks 3 percent registered.

Similar results were confirmed with research on a wide variety of additional programs. Thus, these program planners had good data to suggest that they needed to mail all their brochures a minimum of ten weeks before a program in order to capture the maximum market. As a result of additional study, they found this pattern for the registration response cycle did not repeat itself for all target groups or all programs. The response cycle differed according to occupation. Thus, they were able to adjust the length of time needed between the arrival of the first brochure in a mailbox and the beginning of a program. Depending on the occupation of the target audience, they found that this could vary from three to sixteen weeks.

Tip 171
Plan to collect and summarize your market research so that it can influence your decision making regarding program development.

This is what one organization that conducted over a hundred conferences a year found as a result of analyzing and implementing market research related to program development:

• The actual registration fee for attending a conference or workshop was rarely the critical variable that caused people to register. Employers, almost without exception, paid all registration fees plus travel, lodging, meals, and miscellaneous expenses. As a result, this organization redefined its marketing niche completely. Instead of doing a large number of low or moderately priced programs, they decided to specialize in providing small, elite, and expensive workshops for upper- and top-level management. They dramatically increased fees and decreased the number of programs they were doing in order to concentrate on quality in serving their narrowly but clearly defined new market.

• Location tended to be an important variable that caused their new clientele to register. Therefore, they changed the location of their programs from conference facilities in medium-priced hotels to programs in luxury hotels that had special club floors catering to top management guests.

• The most critical variable affecting registration was whether or not the brochure described in great detail a quality program that emphasized benefits people would receive as a result of attending.

• Another critical variable affecting registration was receiving a long, personal letter, not a printed brochure, describing the program and inviting them to attend. This letter had to be received at least sixteen weeks before each program because their clientele were top-level business people who usually had their calendars already committed six to ten weeks ahead.

• Another variable affecting registration was whether or not people felt that other people like themselves would be attending.

• And the last major variable affecting attendance was whether or not attendees had some role to play in the actual program. As a result of finding this out, the meeting planners redesigned most of their conferences and workshops. They developed swap sessions, small-group discussions led by participant experts, panel presentations, and methods for involving participants in introducing presenters. As a result of these changes, registrations increased and so did satisfaction on program evaluations.

An interesting thing occurred, however, when this organization found that the amount of the registration fee was almost never the critical variable that caused people to attend. The various staff and planning committee members found it difficult to accept this conclusion as valid because it went against their beliefs that low registration fees were essential to attracting more people. Thus, the organization had to design a year-long special strategy to collect additional data and test various levels of registration fees to reconfirm the results of the original research in order to persuade its staff to raise registration fees.

Tip 172
Develop a professional library of market research resources.

Having a professional marketing library on site is invaluable to daily, ongoing research. Such a library should consist of general books related to both quantitative and qualitative research. Of particular help will be books, magazines, and articles dealing with general research techniques as well as research techniques geared directly to issues integral to successful meeting planning. Chapter Eight of this book, which includes a bibliography, provides a comprehensive list of resources to consider.

Summary

The type of action-oriented research described in this chapter is easy to do and does not require the help of external consultants. Planning for this ongoing research function is an important part of building in long-term success for your organization and its programs. It enables you to test program ideas, know your market better, identify the critical variables that affect registration, and design your programs and administrative services so they will be more responsive to your customers' needs. This kind of action-oriented research paves the way for organizational change, innovation, and self-renewal. It is critical to ensuring the long-term success of conferences and workshops.

Exhibit 38. Diagnostic Checklist for
Planning Market Research and Analysis.

This diagnostic checklist summarizes the basic action-oriented research tips presented in this chapter. Reviewing it will help you decide what is working well in your organization and what needs your additional attention. Check your response to each item on the checklist and then develop specific strategies for implementing changes appropriate for your own organization.

Currently effective	Needs some additional work	Major change needed		
____	____	____	1.	How satisfied are you with your general market research efforts?
____	____	____	2.	Do you know the average registration response rate per 1,000 brochures mailed for all your programs?
____	____	____	3.	Have you identified the specific variables that affect registration response rate in your direct-mail advertising?
____	____	____	4.	Have you established reliable tracking systems for all direct-mail brochures?
____	____	____	5.	Do you know exactly what percentage of your budget you spend on marketing activities?
____	____	____	6.	Have you conducted a comprehensive marketing audit of your programs and services?
____	____	____	7.	Have you developed a clear statement of goals you want to achieve with marketing?

Exhibit 38. Diagnostic Checklist for
Planning Market Research and Analysis, Cont'd.

Currently effective	Needs some additional work	Major change needed		
____	____	____	8.	Have you done a comprehensive marketing study of your competition?
____	____	____	9.	Do you know why people do *not* register for your programs?
____	____	____	10.	Do you make active plans for moving all programs through the product life cycle?
____	____	____	11.	Have you done both qualitative and quantitative research on your programs and services during the last year?
____	____	____	12.	Do you have reliable demographic data on your audiences?
____	____	____	13.	Have you developed psychographic data on your audiences?
____	____	____	14.	Do you pilot-test titles for programs in an effort to develop the most attention-getting titles?
____	____	____	15.	Have you used focus groups to assist in your marketing research?

Exhibit 38. Diagnostic Checklist for
Planning Market Research and Analysis, Cont'd.

Currently effective	Needs some additional work	Major change needed		
____	____	____	16.	Have you tested mailing two copies of the same brochure to the same person spaced several weeks apart?
____	____	____	17.	Do you know who pays the registration fee for your participants—individuals or the employer?
____	____	____	18.	Have you conducted split-tests of brochures versus letters to see which draws the most registrants?
____	____	____	19.	Do you keep files containing good, average, and poor examples of direct-mail brochures?
____	____	____	20.	Do you regularly track response times for registrations after a brochure has been mailed?
____	____	____	21.	Have you developed an in-house professional library of market research books, articles, and proven techniques?

Source: Planning and Marketing Conferences and Workshops: Tips, Tools, and Techniques, by Robert G. Simerly. San Francisco: Jossey-Bass. Copyright ©1990. Permission granted to reproduce.

8

Building Professional Knowledge and Skills:

Key Resources and Readings for Conference and Workshop Planners

This chapter provides information on many additional resources helpful to planners of conferences and workshops. For example, included are names, addresses, and telephone numbers of organizations and companies specializing in audiovisual supplies and equipment, computer software, conference supplies, general meeting equipment, films, general office supplies, large and small display systems, promotion supplies, training supplies, visual charts, and control and calendar systems. In addition, there is information on programs to attend for professional development, sources for marketing information, organizations to join, and a bibliography.

A letter, postcard, or phone call to these organizations will bring you complete information about their products and services.

Audiovisual Supplies and Equipment

The following organizations offer a wide variety of audiovisual supplies and equipment. These include such items as sound systems, podiums, slide and overhead projectors, laser pointers, slide makers, television monitors, and easels.

Davson, Division of Eldon Industries, Inc.
1047 Ardmore
Itasca, IL 60143
Telephone: (312) 250–7200

Demco
P.O. Box 7488
Madison, WI 53707
Telephone: (800) 356–8394

Eastman Kodak Company
Rochester, NY 14650
Telephone: (800) 237–5398

General Parametrics
1250 Ninth Street
Berkeley, CA 94710
Telephone: (415) 524–3950

The Highsmith Co., Inc.
W5527 Highway 106
P.O. Box 800
Fort Atkinson, WI 53538–0800
Telephone: (414) 563–9571

Polaroid Corporation
P.O. Box 5011
Clifton, NJ 07015–9919
Telephone: (800) 422–9001

Quartet Ovonics
Quartet Plaza
5700 Old Orchard Road
Skokie, IL 60077
Telephone: (312) 965–0600

RMF Products, Inc.
1275 Paramount Parkway
P.O. Box 520
Batavia, IL 60510
Telephone: (312) 879–0020

3M Audio Visual Department
3M Center
St. Paul, MN 55144–1000
Telephone: (612) 733–1110

Varitronic Systems, Inc.
P.O. Box 234
Minneapolis, MN 55440–9043
Telephone: (800) 637–5461

Visual Horizons
180 Metro Park
Rochester, NY 14623-2666
Telephone: (716) 424-5300

Weyel International
110 East Atlantic Avenue
Delray Beach, FL 33444
Telephone: (407) 276-3082

The Winstead Corporation
10901 Hampshire Avenue South
Minneapolis, MN 55438
Telephone: (800) 447-2257

Computer Software

The following organizations specialize in computer software helpful for handling program registrations, including the production of name badges, rosters, and acknowledgment letters. They also offer integrated accounting packages to manage income and expenses. Since computer software and software firms change so rapidly, it is advisable to collect all of the literature from these firms and review it carefully to determine whether the applications will meet your needs.

Channelmark Corporation
P.O. Box 7600
San Mateo, CA 94403
Telephone: (800) 523-6982

General Parametrics
1250 Ninth Street
Berkeley, CA 94710
Telephone: (415) 524-3950

Group 1 Software
Washington Capital Office Park
6406 Ivy Lane
Suite 500
Greenbelt, MD 20770-1400
Telephone: (800) 368-5806

Intellectual Software
562 Boston Avenue
Bridgeport, CT 06610
Telephone: (800) 232-2224

National Decision System
539 Encinitas Boulevard
P.O. Box 9007
Encinitas, CA 92024–9007
Telephone: (619) 942–7000

Odesta Corporation
4084 Commercial Avenue
Northbrook, IL 60062
Telephone: (800) 323–5423

Peopleware
1715 114th Avenue S.E.
Suite 212
Bellevue, WA 98004
Telephone: (206) 454–6444

Power Up! Software Corporation
P.O. Box 7600
San Mateo, CA 94403
Telephone: (800) 851–2917 (or, in California)
            (800) 223–1479

Paul A. Randle and Associates
986 Sumac Drive
Logan, UT 84321
Telephone: (801) 753–7044

Silton-Bookman Systems
20410 Town Center Lane
Suite 280
Cupertino, CA 95014
Telephone: (408) 446–1170

Topitzes and Associates
6401 Odana Road
Madison, WI 53719
Telephone: (608) 273–4300

Conference Supplies

These organizations produce many products useful for conferences, institutes, workshops, and meetings. They include such items as professionally designed registration packets, notebooks, pens, name badge holders, banners, certificates, awards, trophies, and forms for managing work flow. Each of these organizations will be happy to send you their catalogues, which can become an important part of your professional library.

American Thermoplastic Company
622 Second Avenue
Pittsburgh, PA 15219-2086
Telephone: (800) 245-6600

Artline Industries
3091 Governors Lake Drive
Norcross, GA 30071
Telephone: (404) 446-2500

The Award Company of America
3200 Rice Mine Road
P.O. Box 2029
Tuscaloosa, AL 35403
Telephone: (800) 633-5953

Badge A Minit
48 North 30th Road
Box 800
LaSalle, IL 61301
Telephone: (800) 223-4103

The Banner Barn
P.O. Box 2121
Ocala, FL 32678
Telephone: (904) 867-7860

Best Impressions
348 N. 30th Road
P.O. Box 800
LaSalle, IL 61301
Telephone: (815) 223-6263

Caddylak Systems, Inc.
201 Montrose Road
P.O. Box 1817
Westbury, NY 11590-1768
Telephone: (516) 333-8221

Crestline Co., Inc.
22 West 21st Street
New York, NY 10010
Telephone: (800) 221-7797

DesignerPak Division of Gaylord
P.O. Box 4901
Syracuse, NY 13221-4901
Telephone: (800) 448-6160

Dilley Manufacturing Co.
215 East Third Street
Des Moines, IA 50309
Telephone: (800) 247-5087

Dinn Brothers, Inc.
P.O. Box 111
Holyoke, MA 01041-9981
Telephone: (800) 628-9657

DVC Industries
1440 Fifth Avenue
Bay Shore, NY 11706
Telephone: (516) 968-8500

Full-Color Graphics, Inc.
171 New Highway, N.
Amityville, NY 11701
Telephone: (800) 323-5452

General Binding Corporation
One GBC Plaza
Northbrook, IL 60062
Telephone: (800) 422-7587

Gentile Brothers Screen Printing
116-A High Street
P.O. Box 429
Edinburg, VA 22824
Telephone: (800) 368-5270

Graphic City, Inc.
8648 Dakota Drive
Gaithersburg, MD 20877
Telephone: (301) 975-1070

Heritage Business Forms, Inc.
P.O. Box 2607
Virginia Beach, VA 23450
Telephone: (800) 852-3576

Hoffman & Hoffman
P.O. Box 896
Carmel, CA 93921-0896
Telephone: (800) 227-5813

Johnson Cover Co.
P.O. Box 331
Houston, TX 77001
Telephone: (800) 231-0064

Kruysman, Inc.
160 Varick Street
New York, NY 10013-1269
Telephone: (212) 255-1144

NSC International
Hot Springs, AR 71902-1800
Telephone: (800) 331-5295

Presenta Plaque
P.O. Box 48
Ronkonkoma, NY 11779
Telephone: (800) 824-2930

Sales Guides, Inc.
10510 North Port Washington Road
Mequon, WI 53092-9986
Telephone: (800) 352-9899

TEMPbadge
P.O. Box 659
Spring Valley, NY 10977-0659
Telephone: (800) 628-0022

20th Century Plastics
3628 Crenshaw Blvd.
Los Angeles, CA 90016
Telephone: (800) 421-4662

Vinyl Industrial Products, Inc.
1700 Dobbs Road
St. Augustine, FL 32086-5223
Telephone: (800) 874-0855

Vulcan Binder & Cover Co.
P.O. Box 29
Vincent, AL 35178
Telephone: (800) 633-4526

Professional Development Conferences, Workshops, and Meetings

Among other services, the following organizations offer conferences, workshops, conventions, and annual meetings that can be helpful for the continuing professional development of meeting planners. A letter to them will put you on their mailing list to receive announcements of their upcoming professional development programs.

American Association of Adult and Continuing Education
1201 Sixteenth Street, N.W.
Suite 230
Washington, D.C. 20036
Telephone: (202) 822-7866
They have regional and annual conferences plus additional workshops throughout the year.

American Demographics Institute
P.O. Box 68
Ithaca, NY 14851
Telephone: (800) 828-1133
ADI offers workshops plus annual meetings.

American Society for Training and Development
1630 Duke Street
P.O. Box 1443
Alexandria, VA 22313
Telephone: (703) 683-8100
They offer an annual conference for professionals in training and development.

Clemson University Office of Professional Development
P.O. Drawer 912
Clemson, SC 29633
Telephone: (803) 656-2200
They offer a two-day workshop on increasing registrations through direct mail.

Collegiate Conferences, Inc.
2150 W. 29th Avenue
Suite 500
Denver, CO 80211
Telephone: (303) 433-1200
    This organization provides a number of services designed to match up providers of conferences with prospective clients.

Learning Resources Network
1554 Hayes Drive
Manhattan, KS 66502
Telephone: (913) 539-5376
    LERN offers several workshops each year devoted to marketing and planning of meetings.

The Marketing Federation
7141 Gulf Boulevard
St. Petersburg, FL 33706
Telephone: (813) 367-4934
    They offer a wide variety of workshops related to meeting planning.

Meeting Planners International, INFOMART
1950 Stemmons Freeway
Dallas, TX 75207
Telephone: (214) 746-5222
    They offer conferences for professional meeting planners.

National University Continuing Education Association
One Dupont Circle
Suite 420
Washington, D.C. 20036-1168
Telephone: (202) 659-3130
    NUCEA offers regional and national conferences plus other workshops sponsored with universities.

Professional Convention Management Association
100 Vestavia Office Park
Suite 220
Birmingham, AL 35216
    This organization provides a wide variety of services related to managing conventions.

Resources for Organizations, Inc.
6440 Flying Cloud Drive
Suite 130
Eden Prairie, MN 55344
Telephone: (612) 829-1960

They offer workshops especially designed to enhance presentation techniques at programs.

The Sony Institute of Applied Video Technology
2021 N. Western Avenue
P.O. Box 29906
Los Angeles, CA 90029
Telephone: (213) 462–1987
    Sony offers workshops on video technology related to meeting planning.

TeleCon, Applied Business TeleCommunications
P.O. Box 5106
San Ramon, CA 94583
Telephone: (800) 829–3400
    TeleCon offers workshops on video technology and teleconferencing.

Equipment

These suppliers specialize in many different types of equipment useful in a meeting planning office. For example, these organizations offer everything from routine office furniture, to mailing room equipment, to signs. They will be happy to send you their catalogues.

W. A. Charnstrom Co.
10901 Hampshire Avenue South
Minneapolis, MN 55439
Telephone: (800) 328–2962

Currier-Seedburo Manufacturing Co.
6237 Penn Avenue South
Minneapolis, MN 55423
Telephone: (612) 866–8135

Dispensa-Matic Label Dispensers
725 N. 23rd Street
St. Louis, MO 63103–1500
Telephone: (800) 325–7303

Fox Laminating Company, Inc.
570 New Park Avenue
West Hartford, CT 06110
Telephone: (800) 433–2468

General Binding Corporation
One GBC Plaza
Northbrook, IL 60062
Telephone: (800) 342–5422

Hunley & Packard, Inc.
Rt. 4, Box 601–Dept. MBB
Clinton, TN 37716
Telephone: (615) 457-5060

Kroy, Inc.
Scottsdale Airpark
P.O. Box C–4300
Scottsdale, AZ 85261-4300
Telephone: (602) 948-2222

Master Addresser Company
7506 W. 27th Street
Minneapolis, MN 55426
Telephone: (800) 328-1821

Micro Sign International, Inc.
1001 N. W. 62nd Street
Suite 208
Fort Lauderdale, FL 33309
Telephone: (305) 772-4877

Southern Imperial, Inc.
5600 Pike Street
P.O. Box 2308
Rockford, IL 61131
Telephone: (815) 877-7041

Varitronic Systems, Inc.
300 Interchange Tower
600 South County Rd. 18
Minneapolis, MN 55426
Telephone: (800) 637-5461

Films

Need films or videotapes for training and development activities? Send for these catalogues. In addition, many universities offer film libraries where you can rent both films and tapes on a wide variety of topics.

American Media Incorporated
1454 30th Street
West Des Moines, IA 50625
Telephone: (800) 262-2557

Coronet/MTI Film & Video
108 Wilmot Road
Deerfield, IL 60015
Telephone: (800) 621-2131

CRM Business Films
2233 Faraday
Carlsbad, CA 92008
Telephone: (800) 421-0833

Dartnell
4600 Ravenswood Avenue
Chicago, IL 60640
Telephone: (800) 621-5463

etc. Excellence in Training Corporation
8364 Hickman Road
Suite A
Des Moines, IA 50322
Telephone: (515) 276-6569

Films Incorporated
5547 N. Ravenswood Avenue
Chicago, IL 60640-1199
Telephone: (800) 323-4222

Henson Associates, Inc.
117 E. 69th Street
New York, NY 10021
Telephone: (212) 794-2400

Rank Roundtable Training
113 N. San Vicente Boulevard
Beverly Hills, CA 90211
Telephone: (800) 332-4444

Salenger Films, Inc.
1635 Twelfth Street
Santa Monica, CA 90404
Telephone: (213) 450-1300

Telephone "Doctor" Telephone Techniques–Training Films
12119 St. Charles Rock Road
St. Louis, MO 63044
Telephone: (800) 882-9911

University Associates, Inc.
8517 Production Avenue
San Diego, CA 92121
Telephone: (619) 578-5900

Vantage Communications, Inc.
P.O. Box 546
Nyack, NY 10960
Telephone: (914) 358-0147

Video Arts Inc.
4088 Commercial Avenue
Northbrook, IL 60062-1829
Telephone: (800) 553-0091

Video F.I.N.D.S.
P.O. Box 9497
Dept. 611
New Haven, CT 06534-0497
Telephone: (800) 443-7359

General Office Supplies

An office that is planning conferences and workshops needs a wide variety of general office supplies. Check with your local office supply stores. In addition, these organizations will send you their catalogues so you can shop by mail.

Business Envelope Manufacturers, Inc.
900 Grand Boulevard
Deer Park, Long Island, NY 11729
Telephone: (800) 645-5235

Chiswick Trading, Inc.
33 Union Avenue
Sudbury, MA 01776-0907
Telephone: (800) 225-8708

Colwell Systems, Inc.
201 Kenyon Road
P.O. Box 4025
Champaign, IL 61820-1325
Telephone: (800) 248-7000

Copi-Eze Inc.
P.O. Box 64785
St. Paul, MN 55164-0785
Telephone: (800) 843-0414

Demco
Box 7488
Madison, WI 53707
Telephone: (800) 356-1200

The Highsmith Co., Inc.
W5527 Highway 106
P.O. Box 800
Fort Atkinson, WI 53538-0800
Telephone: (800) 558-2110

Nationwide Printing Inc.
5906 Jefferson Street
Burlington, KY 41005
Telephone: (605) 586-9005

Quill Corporation
100 S. Schelter Road
P.O. Box 4700
Lincolnshire, IL 60197-4700
Telephone: (312) 634-4850

Seton Name Plate Company
P.O. Box LC-1331
New Haven, CT 06505
Telephone: (203) 488-8059

The Stationery House, Inc.
1000 Florida Avenue
Hagerstown, MD 21741
Telephone: (800) 638-3033

UARCO Office Products
121 N. Ninth Street
DeKalb, IL 60115
Telephone: (800) 435-0713

Visible
3626 Stern Avenue
St. Charles, IL 60174
Telephone: (800) 323-0628

Large Display Systems

Interested in designing a large display system for use during your programs? These organizations offer large modular display systems that can be folded up for convenient storage and carrying. In addition, they can provide graphic design service for designing your display system.

Channel-Kor Systems, Inc.
P.O. Box 2297
Bloomington, IN 47402
Telephone: (800) 242-6567

David Brace Displays, Inc.
11600 Genessee Street
Alden, NY 14004
Telephone: (716) 937-9187

The Escort Display Corporation
5739 Howard Street
Niles, IL 60648
Telephone: (800) 323-4333

EuroFrame Portable Display Systems
141 Lanza Avenue
Garfield, NJ 07026
Telephone: (800) 233-8412

ExpoSystems
3203 Queen Palm Drive
Tampa, FL 33619
Telephone: (800) 237-4531

Featherlite Exhibits
7312 32nd Avenue N.
Minneapolis, MN 55427
Telephone: (800) 328-4827

GEM System
2260 South 3600 West
Salt Lake City, UT 84119
Telephone: (801) 974-5616

Glenn Godfrey Communications, Inc.
P.O. Box 10247
Raleigh, NC 27605
Telephone: (919) 782-7914

International Exhibits, Inc.
3625 N. Mississippi Avenue
Portland, OR 97227
Telephone: (800) 331-6633

Iver Display Systems Ltd.
110 Pennsylvania Avenue
Bangor, PA 18013
Telephone: (215) 588-7255

Midland Professional Displays
P.O. Box 247
Atlantic, IA 50022
Telephone: (712) 243-4344

Perrygraf
19365 Business Center Drive
Northridge, CA 91324-3552
Telephone: (800) 423-5329

Professional Displays, Inc.
738 Arrowgrand Circle
Covina, CA 91722
Telephone: (800) 222-6838

Shotel Displays
301 Chestnut Street
St. Paul, MN 55102
Telephone: (612) 222-7317

Skyline Displays, Inc.
12345 Portland Ave. S.
Burnsville, MN 55337-1585
Telephone: (800) 328-2725

TechExhibit, Technical Exhibits Corporation
6155 South Oak Park Avenue
Chicago, IL 60638
Telephone: (312) 586-3377

Small Display Systems and Literature Racks

These organizations specialize in small display racks and systems for displaying literature about your organization and its programs.

Beemak Plastics
7424 Santa Monica Boulevard
Los Angeles, CA 90046
Telephone: (800) 421–4393

Color Optic Literature Displays
5660 Corporate Way
West Palm Beach, FL 33407–2065
Telephone: (800) 327–0477

Demco
P.O. Box 7488
Madison, WI 53707
Telephone: (800) 356–1200

DM Products, Inc.
6721 N. W. 16th Terrace
Fort Lauderdale, FL 33309
Telephone: (305) 978–9100

MD Marketing Displays, Inc.
24450 Indoplex Circle
P.O. Box 576
Farmington Hills, MI 48018–6897
Telephone: (800) 228–8925

Siegel Display Products
P.O. Box 95
Minneapolis, MN 55440
Telephone: (612) 340–1493

Skyline Displays
12345 Portland Avenue South
Burnsville, MN 55337–1585
Telephone: (800) 328–2725

Sutton Designs, Inc.
300 North Tioga
Ithaca, NY 14850
Telephone: (607) 277–4301

Taymar Industries, Inc.
10315 Los Alamitos Boulevard
Los Alamitos, CA 90720
Telephone: (213) 430–7517

Magazines

The following periodicals and companies will help program planners stay abreast of current ideas in the field.

Advertising Age
965 E. Jefferson Avenue
Detroit, MI 48207–9966

Association Management
American Society of Association Executives
1575 I Street, N.W.
Washington, D.C. 20005

AV Video
Montage Publishing, Inc.
25550 Hawthorne Boulevard
Suite 314
Torrance, CA 90505

Business Marketing
22 W. Micheltorena, Suite D
Santa Barbara, CA 93101–9978

Communication Briefings
P.O. Box 587
Glassboro, NJ 08028–0587

Hoke Communications, Inc.
22 W. Micheltorena, Suite D
Santa Barbara, CA 93101–9978

Information Synergy, Inc.
2626 S. Pullman
Santa Ana, CA 92705

Lakewood Publications
50 South Ninth Street
Minneapolis, MN 55402

Marketing Tools Alert
P.O. Box 68
Ithaca, NY 14851

The Meeting Manager
Meeting Planners International
3719 Roosevelt Boulevard
Middletown, OH 45044–6593

Meeting News
Gralla Publications
1515 Broadway
New York, NY 10036

Meetings and Conventions
Murdoch Magazines
News Group Publications
One Park Avenue
New York, NY 10016

Montage Publishing, Inc.
25550 Hawthorne Boulevard, Suite 314
Torrance, CA 90505

Parker Communications Corporation
2801 International Lane, Suite 205
Madison, WI 53704

Presentation Products Magazine
513 Wilshire Blvd., Suite 344
Santa Monica, CA 90401

Sales & Marketing Management Magazine
P.O. Box 1024
Southeastern, PA 19398–9974

Successful Meetings
Bill Communications, Inc.
633 Third Avenue
New York, NY 10017

Telecom: Teleconferencing Newsletter
Center for Interactive Programs
Lowell Hall
610 Langdon Street
Madison, WI 53703

TeleProfessional
P.O. Box 2381
Waterloo, IA 50704

Training and Development Journal
1630 Duke Street
P.O. Box 1443
Alexandria, VA 22313

Training: Magazine of HRD
731 Hennepin Avenue
Minneapolis, MN 55403

Who's Mailing What!
P.O. Box 8180
Stamford, CT 06905

Promotion Supplies

Promotion supplies are often appropriate for meetings. These organizations will send you their literature on promotion supplies covering everything from key chains, calendars, and pens to embossed candy, laminated luggage tags, and keepsake souvenirs.

Art Poly Bag Company
140 Metropolitan Avenue
Brooklyn, NY 11211
Telephone: (718) 388-0866

Atlas Pen & Pencil Corporation
3040 N. 29th Avenue
P.O. Box 600
Hollywood, FL 33022-0600

B & B Advertising
P.O. Box 220, Dept. 90
Scott City, KS 67871
Telephone: (800) 835-0002

Best Impressions
348 N. 30th Road
P.O. Box 800
LaSalle, IL 61301
Telephone: (815) 223-6263 or
             (800) 635-2378

California Cachet
300 Brannan Street, Suite 303
San Francisco, CA 94107
Telephone: (415) 777-1000

First Minnesota Pen, Inc.
123 North Third Street
Minneapolis, MN 55401
Telephone: (612) 333–3996

Gift Service, Inc.
35 Winthrop Avenue
Birmingham, AL 35213
Telephone: (205) 879–4438

Graphics, Inc.
1400 Indiantown Road
P.O. Box 937
Jupiter, FL 33468
Telephone: (407) 746–6746

Graphics3
1400 Indiantown Road
P.O. Box 937
Jupiter, FL 33468
Telephone: (407) 746–6746

Herff Jones, Inc.
1411 N. Capitol Avenue
P.O. Box 687
Indianapolis, IN 46206
Telephone: (317) 635–1554

Idea Craft
1350 Old Skokie Road
Highland Park, IL 60035
Telephone: (312) 831–4720

Limited Editions
1006 S. Michigan Avenue
Chicago, IL 60605
Telephone: (312) 341–1920

Marketing Bulletin Board
22 W. Micheltorena, Suite D
Santa Barbara, CA 93101
Telephone: (805) 687–3137

Martguild, Inc.
576 Industrial Parkway

P.O. Box 382
Chagrin Falls, OH 44022
Telephone: (216) 247-8978

Nelson Marketing, Inc.
P.O. Box 840
611 North Street
Logansport, IN 46947-0840
Telephone: (219) 722-5203

Ovation Awards
44 Lehigh Avenue
Paterson, NJ 07503
Telephone: (201) 345-1008

Positive Promotions
222 Ashland Place
Brooklyn, NY 11217
Telephone: (718) 858-4199

Sales Guides, Inc.
10510 North Port Washington Road
Mequon, WI 53092-9986
Telephone: (800) 352-9899

Screen Gems
P.O. Box 140
Fort Montgomery, NY 10922
Telephone: (800) 345-8486

Siegel Advertising Specialties & Business Gifts
P.O. Box 95
Minneapolis, MN 55440
Telephone: (612) 340-1493

World's Finest Chocolate, Inc.
4801 S. Lawndale
Chicago, IL 60632-3062
Telephone: (312) 847-4600

Visual Charts and Control and Calendar Systems

Visual charts and control and calendar systems may be needed in your office to help monitor your many activities. If so, send for these catalogues for the latest information of what is available in this area.

Abbot Office Systems
6 Asbury Avenue
Framingdale, NJ 07727
Telephone: (800) 631-2233

Baldwin Cooke
2401 Waukegan Road
Deerfield, IL 60015
Telephone: (312) 948-7600

Caddylak Systems, Inc.
201 Montrose Road
P.O. Box 1817
Westbury, NY 11590-1768
Telephone: (516) 333-8221

Day-Timers, Inc.
One Day-Timer Plaza
Allentown, PA 18195-1551
Telephone: (215) 395-5884

Magna Visual, Inc.
9400 Watson Road
St. Louis, MO 63126-1596
Telephone: (800) 622-6273

Memindex, Inc.
149 Carter Street
Rochester, NY 14601
Telephone: (800) 828-5885

Remarkable Products
245 Pegasus Avenue
Northvale, NJ 07647
Telephone: (201) 784-0900

Helpful Organizations

There are many organizations that can be helpful to program planners. A letter to them will bring a complete description of the organization, its services, and its benefits.

American Association for Adult and Continuing Education
1601 Sixteenth Street, N.W.
Washington, D.C. 20036

American Hotel and Motel Association
888 Seventh Avenue
New York, NY 10019

American Society for Training and Development
1630 Duke Street
P.O. Box 1443
Alexandria, VA 22313

American Society of Association Executives
1575 I Street, N.W.
Washington, D.C. 20005

Association of Group Travel Executives, Inc.
320 East 58th Street
New York, NY 10022

Convention Liaison Council
1575 I Street, N.W.
Suite 1200
Washington, D.C. 20005

Council of Engineering and Scientific Society Executives
2000 Florida Avenue, N.W.
Washington, D.C. 20009

Exhibit Designers and Producers Association
60 East 42nd Street
New York, NY 10017

Exposition Service Contractors Association
1516 South Pontius Avenue
Los Angeles, CA 90025

Foundation for International Meetings
1400 K Street, N.W., Number 750
Washington, D.C. 20005

Health Care Exhibitors Association
5775 Peachtree-Dunwoody Road, Suite 500-D
Atlanta, GA 30342

Hotel Sales and Marketing Association International
1400 K Street, N.W., Suite 810
Washington, D.C. 20005

Institute of Association Management Companies
5820 Wilshire Boulevard, Suite 500
Los Angeles, CA 90036

Insurance Conference Planners Association
c/o Equitable Life Insurance Co.
1285 Avenue of the Americas
New York, NY 10019

International Association of Auditorium Managers
500 North Michigan Avenue, Suite 1400
Chicago, IL 60611

International Association of Conference Centers
900 South Highway Drive
Fenton, MO 63026

International Association of Convention and Visitors Bureaus
1809 Woodfield Drive
Savoy, IL 61874

International Association of Fairs and Expositions
P.O. Box 985
Springfield, MO 65801

International Conference of Industry Associations
1400 K Street, N.W., Suite 750
Washington, D.C. 20005

International Congress and Convention Association
J. W. Brouswerplein 27
P.O. Box 5343
Amsterdam, The Netherlands

International Exhibitors Association
5103-B Backlick Road
Annandale, VA 22003

International Hotel Association
110 East 59th Street, Suite 900
New York, NY 10022

Meeting Planners International
1950 Stemmons Freeway
Dallas, TX 75207

National Association of Exposition Managers
P.O. Box 377
Aurora, OH 44202

National Passenger Traffic Association
310 Madison Avenue
Room 420
New York, NY 10017

National University Continuing Education Association
Conferences and Institutes Division
One Dupont Circle, N.W., Suite 420
Washington, D.C. 20036–1168

Professional Convention Management Association
2027 First Avenue North
Suite 1007, Commerce Center
Birmingham, AL 35203

Religion Convention Managers Association
205 Enid Lane
Northfield, IL 60093

Religious Conference Management Association
One Hoosier Dome, Suite 120
Indianapolis, IN 46225

Society of Company Meeting Planners
2600 Garden Road, Suite 208
Monterey, CA 93940

Society of Government Meeting Planners
1133 15th Street, N.W.
Washington, D.C. 20005

Society of Incentive Travel Executives
271 Madison Avenue
New York, NY 10016

Assistance with Meeting Site Selection

The following publications are helpful in assisting with site selection.

Arena Stadium Guide
Amusement Business
Box 24970
Nashville, TN 37202

Conference Services Directory
Association of College and University Housing Officers
Central Support Services Office
101 Curl Drive
Columbus, OH 43210–1195

Conference Facilities and Services Directory
National University Continuing Education Association
One Dupont Circle, Suite 615
Washington, D.C. 20036

Gavel — Meetings and Conventions
Murdoch Magazines
News Group Publications
One Park Avenue
New York, NY 10016

Hotel and Motel Red Book
American Hotel Association Directory Corporation
888 Seventh Avenue
New York, NY 10019

Meeting News
Gralla Publications
1515 East 55th Street
New York, NY 10039

Membership Directory
International Association of Conference Centers
900 South Highway Drive
Fenton, MO 63026

National Hotel Information Center
155 East 55th Street
New York, NY 10039

Official Hotel and Resort Guide
P.O. Box 5800
Cherry Hill, NJ 08034

Successful Meetings — Facilities Directory
Bill Communications, Inc.
633 Third Avenue
New York, NY 10017

Bibliography

The books in this section are directly related to the planning and marketing of conferences and workshops.

Adam, H. *Meetings, Conventions, and Incentive Travel: 4349 Ideas and Money-Saving Tips.* Jenkintown, Pa.: Helen Adam & Associates, 1985.

Alles, A. *Exhibitions: Universal Marketing Tools.* New York: Wiley, 1974.

American Society of Association Executives. *Guidelines for Effective Association Conventions and Meetings.* Washington, D.C.: American Society of Association Executives, 1978.

Auger, B. Y. *How to Run Better Business Meetings: An Executive's Guide to Meetings That Get Things Done.* St. Paul, Minn.: 3M Company, 1979.

Bradford, L. P. *Making Meetings Work: A Guide for Leaders and Group Members.* San Diego, Calif.: University Associates, 1976.

Burke, W. W., and Beckhard, R. (eds.). *Conference Planning.* (2nd ed.) Alexandria, Va.: NTL Institute, 1970.

Burnett, E. *The Complete Direct-Mail List Handbook.* Englewood Cliffs, N.J.: Prentice-Hall, 1988.

Caddylak Systems. *You Can Organize a Successful Meeting—Large or Small.* Westbury, N.Y.: Caddylak Systems, 1985.

Cavalier, R. *Achieving Objectives in Meetings.* Chicago: Program Counsel, 1973.

Chapman, E. A., Jr. *Exhibit Marketing: A Survival Guide for Managers.* New York: McGraw-Hill, 1987.

Cooper, S., and Heenan, C. *Preparing, Designing and Leading Workshops.* New York: CBI Publishing, 1979.

Davis, L. N., and McCallon, E. *Planning and Evaluating Workshops.* Austin, Tex.: Learning Concepts, 1975.

Desatnick, R. L. *Managing to Keep the Customer: How to Achieve and Maintain Superior Customer Service Throughout the Organization.* San Francisco: Jossey-Bass, 1987.

Dieffenderfer, R. A., Kopp., L., and Cap, O. *Workshops.* Columbus, Ohio: National Center for Research in Vocational Education, 1977.

Dobmeyer, E. *Registration Techniques to Increase Enrollments.* Manhattan, Kans.: Learning Resources Network, 1986.

Drain, R. *Successful Conference and Convention Planning.* New York: McGraw-Hill, 1978.

Draves, W. A. *Marketing Techniques for Office Staff.* Manhattan, Kans.: Learning Resources Network, 1986.

Dubey, R. E., and others. *A Practical Guide for Dynamic Conferences.* Lanham, Md.: University Press of America, 1982.

Eitington, J. E. *The Winning Trainer.* Houston, Tex.: Gulf, 1984.

Elliott, R. D. *Mailing Lists: How to Build and Maintain a High-Quality Mailing List.* Manhattan, Kans.: Learning Resources Network, 1982.

Elliott, R. D. *Marketing In-House Seminars.* Manhattan, Kans.: Learning Resources Network, 1986.

Elliott, R. D. *House Lists: How to Create a More Responsive In-House List.* Manhattan, Kans.: Learning Resources Network, 1987.

Falk, C. F., and Miller, P. *Market Research in Adult Learning.* Manhattan, Kans.: Learning Resources Network, 1986.

Farlow, H. *Publicizing and Promoting Programs.* New York: McGraw-Hill, 1979.

Ferrel, R. *Field Manager's Guide to Successful Meetings.* New York: Successful Meetings, 1977.

Finkel, C. *Professional Guide to Successful Meetings.* New York: Successful Meetings, 1976.

Fischer, R. B. *Personal Contact in Marketing.* Manhattan, Kans.: Learning Resources Network, 1984.

Freedman, L. *Quality in Continuing Education: Principles, Practices, and Standards for Colleges and Universities.* San Francisco: Jossey-Bass, 1987.

Gram, R. *Direct Mail Workshop: 1,001 Ideas, Tips, Rule Breakers, and Brainstorms for Improving Profits Fast.* Englewood Cliffs, N.J.: Prentice-Hall, 1989.

Harper, R. *Mailing List Strategies: A Guide to Direct-Mail Success.* New York: McGraw-Hill, 1986.

Hon, D. C. *Meetings That Matter.* Austin, Tex.: Learning Concepts, 1980.

How to Participate Profitably in Trade Shows. (2nd ed.) Rochester, N.Y.: Dartnell, n.d.

Ilsley, P. J. (ed.). *Improving Conference Design and Outcomes.* New Directions for Continuing Education, no. 28. San Francisco: Jossey-Bass, 1985.

Jeffries, J. R., and Bates, J. D. *The Executive's Guide to Meetings, Conferences, and Audiovisual Presentations.* New York: McGraw-Hill, 1982.

Jones, J. E. *Meeting Management: A Professional Approach.* (Rev. ed.) Stamford, Conn.: Bayard Publications, 1984.

Jones, M. *How to Organize Meetings: A Handbook for Better Workshop, Seminar, and Conference Management.* New York: Kampmann, 1981.

Kirkpatrick, D. L. *How to Plan and Conduct Productive Business Meetings.* Rochester, N.Y.: Dartnell, 1976.

Knox, A. B. *Helping Adults Learn: A Guide to Planning, Implementing, and Conducting Programs.* San Francisco: Jossey-Bass, 1986.

Laric, M. V., and Stiff, R. *VISICALC for Marketing and Sales.* Englewood Cliffs, N.J.: Prentice-Hall, 1984.

Leffel, G. *Designing Brochures for Results.* Manhattan, Kans.: Learning Resources Network, 1983.

Lenz, E. *Creating and Marketing Programs in Continuing Education.* New York: McGraw-Hill, 1980.

Leroux, P. *Selling to a Group: Presentation Strategies.* New York: Harper & Row, 1984.

Library of Sales Conference Ideas. Monterey Park, Calif.: Sales Communication, 1977.

Mandel, S. *Effective Presentation Skills*. Los Altos, Calif.: Crisp Publications, 1987.

Meeting Planners International. *Meeting Professionals Handbook*. Middletown, Ohio: Meeting Planners International, 1985.

Meeting Planning Institute. *The Meeting and Convention Publicity Kit*. Ft. Washington, Pa.: Meeting Planning Institute, 1985.

Mitchell, A. *The Nine American Lifestyles: Who We Are and Where We Are Going*. New York: Warner Books, 1983.

Munson, L. *How to Conduct Training Seminars*. New York: McGraw-Hill, 1983.

Murray, S. L. *How to Organize and Manage a Seminar*. Englewood Cliffs, N.J.: Prentice-Hall, 1983.

Nadler, L. *Designing Training Programs: The Critical Events Model*. Reading, Mass.: Addison-Wesley, 1982.

Nadler, L., and Nadler, Z. *The Conference Book*. Houston, Tex.: Gulf, 1977.

Nadler, L., and Nadler, Z. *The Comprehensive Guide to Successful Conferences and Meetings: Detailed Instructions and Step-by-Step Checklists*. San Francisco: Jossey-Bass, 1987.

Newman, P., and Lynch, A. E. *How to Run an Effective Meeting*. New York: McGraw-Hill, 1979.

Off-Site Meetings. Supplement to *Training Magazine*. Minneapolis: Lakewood Publications, Feb. 1989.

Ostrand, K. *Trips and Tours Manual*. Manhattan, Kans.: Learning Resources Network, 1985.

Oxbridge Directory of Newsletters. New York: Oxbridge Communications, 1989.

Parker, L. A. (ed.). *Teleconferencing Resource Book*. New York: Elsevier Science, 1984.

Patton, M. Q. *Qualitative Evaluation*. Newbury Park, Calif.: Sage, 1980.

Pentland, L. *Salesbook Spreadsheets*. New York: McGraw-Hill, 1985.

Professional Convention Management Association. *Professional Meeting Management: The Complete Guide to Convention and Meeting Planning*. Birmingham, Ala.: Professional Convention Management Association, 1985.

Schindler-Raiman, E., and Lippitt, R. *Taking Your Meetings Out of the Doldrums*. San Diego, Calif.: University Associates/Learning Resources, 1975.

Schrello Direct Marketing. *Marketing In-House Programs*. Long Beach, Calif.: Schrello Direct Marketing, n.d.

Seekings, D. *How to Organize Effective Conferences and Meetings*. (2nd ed.) New York: Nichols, 1984.

Shea, G. *Managing a Difficult or Hostile Audience*. Englewood Cliffs, N.J.: Prentice-Hall, 1984.

Shenson, H. L. *Strategic Seminar and Workshop Marketing*. Manhattan, Kans.: Learning Resources Network, 1985.

Simerly, R. G. *Budgeting for Successful Conferences and Institutes*. Manhattan, Kans.: Learning Resources Network, 1982.

Simerly, R. G. *Successful Budgeting for Conferences and Seminars.* Manhattan, Kans.: Learning Resources Network, 1984.

Simerly, R. G., and Associates. *Strategic Planning and Leadership in Continuing Education: Enhancing Organizational Vitality, Responsiveness, and Identity.* San Francisco: Jossey-Bass, 1987.

Simerly, R. G., and Associates. *Handbook of Marketing for Continuing Education.* San Francisco: Jossey-Bass, 1989.

Sork, T. J. (ed.). *Designing and Implementing Effective Workshops.* New Directions for Continuing Education, no. 22. San Francisco: Jossey-Bass, 1984.

Suleiman, A. S. *Developing and Marketing Successful Seminars and Conferences.* Miami, Fla.: Marketing Federation, 1982.

Techniques for Business Meetings and Presentations. Rochester, N.Y.: Dartnell, 1976.

This, L. *The Small Meeting Planner.* (2nd ed.) Houston, Tex.: Gulf, 1976.

Walker, S. B. *Conference Planning.* Washington, D.C.: National Training and Development Service, 1975.

Wolfson, S. M. *The Meeting Planners' Complete Guide to Negotiating.* Washington, D.C.: Institute for Meeting and Conference Management, 1984.

Annual Publications

Direct-Mail List Rates and Data. Wilmette, Ill.: Standard Rate and Data Service.

The Direct Marketing Market Place: The Directory of the Direct Marketing Industry. Hewlett Harbor, N.Y.: Hilary House Publishers.

Encyclopedia of Associations. Detroit, Mich.: Gale Research.Simerly, R. G. *Successful Budgeting for Conferences and Seminars.* Manhattan, Kans.: Learning Resources Network, 1984.

Index